Hear Us Out

AMAL KOOHEJI
SAJEDA AL ASFOOR

Cover and Interior:
Qamber Designs & Media

TABLE OF CONTENTS

FOREWORD

I found myself reading this book twice within a couple of days... something I rarely do. The second reading was due to my tremendous enjoyment of the first reading and the fact that I liked the way it was written. I felt that the characters are alive and talking *to* me.

The two authors must have put alot of thought and effort to make the storyline so simple to comprehend and easy to follow, yet rich in content and full of new thoughts and perspectives.

When little Thomas Edison was expelled from school at an early age, his mother started home-schooling him. He always admitted that he became the genius that he is and the biggest inventor of all times, because his mother simply believed in him, trusted his abilities and saw that he was simply different!

Millennials are a different breed of people. The generational gaps are a norm in the history of time and are transitional in nature thus very easy to manage; however, the fast development in technology and connectivity has contributed to the largest gap ever witnessed between any two generations in time, which is the gap between millennials who were born when internet already existed and Gen X which witnessed only its beginning. Millennials living in today's world unlike ours, need to be given the same chances, to be believed in and to be listened to. They are born in a time where they can access all information with a push of a button. Millennials are no more tomorrow's leaders, *they are today's leaders*. Let us look around us and we will see that many international conglomerates that have achieved great success are run by them.

Millennials are often misinterpreted by their predecessor generations of Gen X and Baby Boomers. Their attitude and expectations of the workplace are different than others. They are not necessarily wrong but simply different. They are not afraid to question authority and are always looking for new challenges and more satisfying jobs. Job-hopping has become a norm for Gen Y. This should not be taken against them and be frowned upon but on the contrary, job-hopping provides them with a variety of experiences and skills, which we must appreciate.

For a harmonious and efficient workplace, Gen X and Gen Y need to bridge the gap between them and bolster their empathy for each other. They need to complement each other rather than compete. Any successful organisation needs both. Putting themselves in the other's shoes and sincerely listening to each other, with a genuine attempt to see other's point of views from their stance. Nobody is perfect and thus we have to accept each other's shortcomings and rise above them. Millennials appreciate being appraised, reassured, and being kept in the loop. Gen Xers can help in developing their talents and skills.

This book is cleverly and elegantly constructed. You can easily read through the minds of the two generations, therefore giving you a true picture of how they think and feel about each other. It's definitely a book that is well narrated and worth reading in the aim of progressing your workplace and enhancing your productivity.

Abdulelah Ebrahim Al Qassimi
Ex-Founding CEO of Tamkeen
— An empowerment agency that strives to build the nation's people

PREFACE

No man has ever put the reality of generational differences in better words than Gibran Khalil Gibran, who surpassed generations ahead of his time. He taught us the reality of life's procession towards the infinite and that "change" is the *only* constant. The ethos of this book has long been written by him (may his soul rest in peace).

ON CHILDREN
Gibran Khalil Gibran

Your children are not your children.
They are the sons and daughters of Life's longing for itself.
They come through you but not from you,
And though they are with you, yet they belong not to you.
You may give them your love but not your thoughts,
For they have their own thoughts.
You may house their bodies but not their souls,
For their souls dwell in the house of tomorrow,
which you cannot visit, not even in your dreams.
You may strive to be like them,
but seek not to make them like you.
For life goes not backward nor tarries with yesterday.
You are the bows from which your children
as living arrows are sent forth.
The archer sees the mark upon the path of the infinite,
and He bends you with His might
that His arrows may go swift and far.
Let your bending in the archer's hand be for gladness;
For even as He loves the arrow that flies,
so He loves also the bow that is stable.

This is dedicated to all those who dare to change the status quo for the growth of the true value of any organisation—its people.

"When you change the way you look at things, the things you look at change"

— WAYNE DYER

LET'S GET STARTED

W e live in a paradoxical world in which nobody can claim igno-
rance because the entire universe is available to us at a tiny
press of the 'virtual" gateway—our phones—which have now
become the windows of our minds and lives, our present and our future.

This revolution not only shaped our millennials and is responsible for shaping cognitive, social, and behavioural skills of our KG-aged
children, but this revolution has also made us literally and truly live in one
global village to the farthest extent and essence of that term. There are
no informational, social, nor religious barriers to communication when
a group meets and discusses any shared topic from all four corners of
the world. With all its perils on one hand, the pearls which the internet
brings to us and to our economic and social progress undoubtedly far
surpasses the adversities. It has changed our world, our lives, our jobs,
our families, our social structures, our thoughts, and our behaviour. Gen
Xers were at their prime age when this revolution paved its way, but
Gen Y's were much younger and witnessed this wealth of information
at high school. It was a time where this information was growing ever so
rapidly. And its bounties and impact were clearly visible and integrated
in their daily existence.

A conversation between the two generations is thus essential. Gen Ys
are devouring the workforce in unprecedented volumes and speeds,
and Xers are left dismayed since their predecessor baby boomers are
leaving. They have no option but to recruit and motivate millennials who
are wired differently and have astronomical expectations and skill-sets
that far vary from theirs.

Before we talk about the theme of our book—which is the differing
views—there is something deeper to be discussed. Let us talk about *age*
discrimination. This type of partialism has left many Gen Xers declining
work prospects in what was believed would be the most prosperous
years of their lives. The young snapchatting, instagramming millenni-

GEN Z
(1998 - NOW)

The Great Recession
War on Terror;
War on Climate Change

Savers, non-drinkers,
non-smokers

Life hackers,
"Let's make it better"

BORN INTO
SURVIVORS

CONSERVATIVE

FIXERS

GREATEST
GENERATION
(1928 - 1946)

The Great Depression
World War II

Strong morals, thrifty,
responsible

MILLENNIALS
(1981-1997)

Generation Me,
Some Gen Z's parents,
Gen Z's older siblings

BABY BOOMERS
(1946 - 1964)

Grandparents of Gen Z,
live in multigenerational
homes with Gen Z

GEN X
(1965-1980)

The middle child of
generations, parents
of Gen Z

als are taking over jobs and the world. Baby boomers are retiring, and where are Gen Xers in this equation? They are left in the shadows.

On the other hand, millennials are indeed facing challenges. Unemployment rates for young workers are the highest since World War II. Each generation blames the other—the older blaming the younger for being able to work longer hours at a fraction of the cost and consequently taking over, while the younger blaming the older for delaying retirement and clogging the employment and recruitment of youth in the p peline. Unfortunately, this intergenerational tension based on age discrimination will worsen as the age gap widens. However, this diversity is at the core of the development of entrepreneurial organisations. Some countries celebrate this diversity and have built societal "multi-generational houses" whereby people of different ages get together to benefit from this gap.

There are undeniably fundamental differences in managing these varying generations. Call it generation discrimination or not, it all boils down to priorit es. We need people who produce, yet we don't examine in-depth what truly drives people to be comfortable, happy, and productive. Filling the "purpose gap" seems to be the toughest challenge staring in the face of managers today.

This book aims to exhibit candid views coming from two generations. It has been co-authored simply to showcase two genuine views and act as a "call for change". Its theme is universal, yet its context is regional. The Middle-East bears no difference than any other nation in this challenge since youth have all been influenced by one school, one master, one caretaker, one information and values provider—the Internet. HR specialists and managers of today will realize the need for such tips described in this light and brief account of a journey of a millennial in an organisation and her experiences from the day of her interview until she contemplates leaving. Her Gen X mentor also shows us the battle in her own mind about the challenges she faces in achieving the right corporate culture that is productive and positive for the growing Gen Y staff.

HR practitioners and managers of today—Gen X and baby boomers—need to have a peek into this millennial's mind and thought process. This book therefore attempts to unravel her thoughts to you. Coinciding this journey is also the account of a Gen Xer who is faced with the challenge of living in the baby boomer's world and battling with the demands of the new millennial workforce. She takes charge, tries to control her frustrations with this generation, and takes a bold step into trying to empathize, understand, and give this generation a chance to lead the way. She uses a team of her millennial workforce to help her devise a plan for revamping how the organisation should shift from a very traditional one to a forward-thinking, all-embracing one, characterised by flexibility and empowerment.

It is said that "change is the only constant". It is therefore what we are all bound to embark upon. Happy journey.

Chapter One
STEPPING IN

Meet Mrs. Hope

GEN X BORN IN 1972

"*F*eeling dismayed by youth or these so-called millennials—a generation that I have strived hard to nurture and impact with utmost openness and trust. How can we find the balance of meeting our bottom lines if we spend a huge amount of time just keeping them happy and engaged enough to produce the basic minimum? I have just come back from the executive management meeting, trying to convince them *not to* cut budgets for psychometric recruitment tests, the new onboarding programme, training, and team outings because it plays an integral part in identifying high-caliber candidates and retaining them.

The biggest challenge that faces organisations nowadays is hunting for the match whilst being transparent and ensuring the provision of equal opportunities. How can we possibly do that without standards? Standards cannot occur without consistency, which is why training our recruitment teams to assess all candidates equally and impartially is part of our protocol.

It is true that we are known for being pessimistic and cynical, and this is certainly understandable considering that we came in at the brink of the Cold War, saw the fall of the Berlin Wall, experienced revolutions in the Middle East, survived a series of economic crises, and lived through the AIDS epidemic, just to name a few. Raising youth was a hell-raising task as we moved into our middle age. We acquired this overwhelming sense of responsibility to fix the mistakes that our predecessors made in society. We are pragmatic, cunning, and hard to fool because we have seen it all and have come through deep valleys and steep mountains, and those who made it didn't falter because of their great resilience and grit at the workplace. We are the "neglected" middle-child because it seems that all eyes are on the slowly retiring baby boomers or the ascending millennials, now the world's majority generation. Profound research, however, shows that we may be equally capable at digital tasks as millennials and that we show a mastery of conventional leadership skills more on par with leaders of the baby boomer generation. This includes identifying and developing new talent at our organisations and driving the execution of business strategies to bring new ideas to reality. We are adaptable and proven to be more connected and thus have no reason to fret.

I'm thinking about the request of the executive management team, who has finally decided to in-source a lot of front-office functions. They are waiting for a master plan for HR but have appointed me as the leader of this activity because I am known to be an advocate of the people and especially, the youth. I have no idea whether I am up to this challenge since this generation fails me at times. But I will surely need to come up with a wonderful plan that addresses all issues and makes us 'win' in becoming the *employer of choice*.

I walk down the corridor, heavily disappointed with the interviews I just had for three consecutive days for this major in-sourcing project. I'm overwhelmed with the feedback I just heard from my fellow interviewers on other panels. That's when I see a young girl that I met three years ago at a youth conference—one that left a lasting impression and has since communicated regularly for advice and information... the millennial type I would love to hire. My eyes light up when I realise that she just finished her interview in one of the rooms. Approaching her , I ask, 'So Saj, how was your interview with us today?' not knowing what kind of conversation that question would lead to. A battlefield between two generations, one in which I had to skin myself of all my experiences, rid myself of expectations, and try to understand this high-maintenance generation in order to make the right choices and achieve a productive, balanced work environment with such diverse generations within it."

Meet Saj

MILLENNIAL BORN IN 1991

"*S*wimming against the current is the best way to describe how I feel. Keeping my disappointment and frustration under control while pursuing a lifelong dream of mine and chasing after the career I have always dreamt of is harder than I have ever expected. The thought that many organisations still follow the same standardized recruitment format brings me back to my sobering reality. It almost feels as though we are being ridiculed for thinking differently or for expecting simple things such as a modernized workplace environment, which in all honesty is the least that should happen. Not only that, it is the idea that we so-called millennials are lazy and do not have the same drive and ambition as the generation before us, which really winds me up.

There is certainly no denying that we, Generation Y, are the cause of a heated debate between the previous Generation Xers and their ancestor baby boomers. We have been referred to on many occasions as 'lazy, entitled, self-expressive narcissists.' So what aggravates me the most is the need to redress such false stereotypes whenever I am surrounded by older generations. And that is exactly why I am not a fan of traditional interviews. It almost feels like entering a courtroom, perceived to be guilty, pleading before your sentence—

it's nothing but a futile effort aiming to invalidate generalizations!"

It is with extremely mixed emotions that I leave the small meeting room of my highly anticipated job interview. I am baffled by the reality that I was asked exactly the same questions my parents had asked me to rehearse for- questions that I have consciously decided not to deliberate on as I was fairly confident of the 'new' era I was a part of.

'So Saj, how was your interview with us today?'

My train of thought is suddenly interrupted by a familiar voice. I turn around. Little did I know that the conversation I was about to have just then would lead to a ceaseless debate between two generations that simply seemed irreconcilable. It is true what they say: 'A generation gap is a perpetual phenomenon, one that you cannot possibly escape or undo.'

I am suddenly lost in my own thoughts. I am unsure if I should reply truthfully and voice my opinion unapologetically. My heart is telling me not to ruin any chances of potentially getting hired, but my head cannot simply contain all the anger and frustration at the experience I just had. Should I be the one to tell the truth? But then again, if I don't, who will? I cannot stand here and mask my emotions. I cannot wait for someone else to influence change in what is perceived to be a 'modern world of work.' As young and as inexperienced as I may be, I feel a sense of duty. I took the responsibility upon myself and for all the youth that are trying to navigate today's workplace to disrupt the cultural norms and quash outdated notions.

> "Young people need to be asked what matters, not be told what matters"
> — JEFF MARTIN

Frankly speaking, isn't it time to replace the traditional job interview that requires us to answer a set of scripted questions that I could potentially lie to in order to guarantee getting the job? There are many psychological factors that play a part in evaluating the person interviewed and sometimes our unconscious biases conclude the decision by simply looking at the person and evaluating their set skills on no basis whatsoever. Actors audition and so do singers, because you cannot logically ask them how well they can deliver and perform. But the irony is, it is as important to evaluate a prospective sales representative by seeing him/her *sell*. The same applies to web designers, call center agents, journalists, lawyers, you name it. It just makes sense to *audition* a prospective employee before having them sign a job offer. I was extremely frustrated to know that reality simply did not exist. The reality may have been that the interviewer scanned that piece of paper only a few minutes before I stepped into the meeting room. *As if* I can convey any differentiating value and qualities of mine through a mere resume on which I am going to be judged upon."

A generation can essentially be defined as a group identifiable by similarit es in age and notable life even:s at critical developmental stages. The two prominent generational groups that are most pertinent in today's workforce are the millenn als (also known as Generation Y) and Generation X.

Researchers, human resource specialists, employers and managers are increasingly interested in getting the balance right as far as managing and working with people from different generations is concerned. A lot of this interest is fundamentally steeped in the idea that generations have a few subtle and a few significant differences in their values, goals, and expectations in the workplace. In this book, we hope to explore some of those differences and share insights into how some of them can be reconciled to create a cohesive workforce that is tolerant, cooperative, and productive.

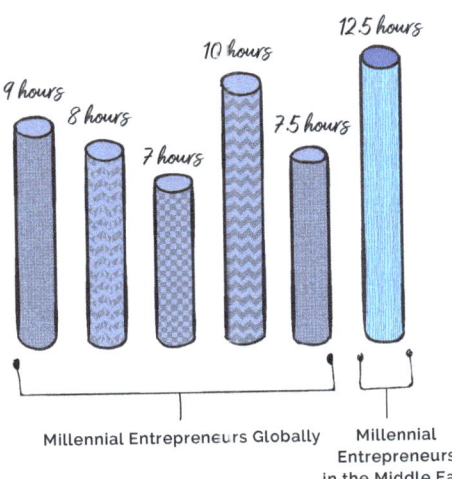

Millennial Entrepreneurs Globally Millennial Entrepreneurs in the Middle East

MILLENNIAL ENTREPRENEURS IN THE MIDDLE EAST SEEM TO WORK THE HARDEST

Their average workday is 12.5 hours, more than 2.5 hours above the global average for millennials. They are the Middle East's greatest asset and their entrepreneurial spirit seems to be shaping the future of the region

SOURCE: Entrepreneurial Creatives, Skeptical — The Truth about MENA Millennials, Chayme Samir, World Economic Forum, 2017

One of the most interesting—and least discussed—ideas about millennials is that they are breaking into twc different generational groups. One group of millennials is reaching all the traditional markers of adulthood, though a few years later than previous generations. This group is working towards careers and entering their wealth accumulation life phase, commanding more power in the workplace. The other group of millennials, however, is not creating "real-world traction." This is the group you've probably heard most about—the ones that still live at home and let mom pay their cell phone bill.

By the time millennials reach age 30, they will self-select into one group or the other and can no longer relate to the other segment of their generation. These divergent trajectories will have profound implications for the workforce, marketplace, government, economy, and more. In fact, the group most offended by millennials who act entitled, is other millennials who do *not* feel entitled. The unentitled millennials think that the rest of the generation gives them a bad reputation.

Gen X Speaking

Gen Xers are characterized by individuality and independence, so when being recruited, we tend to care a lot about the scope of our own work and accountability. I'm concerned about how I fit into the whole picture, because interdependence means fitting into a project seamlessly with others to produce a worthy whole. That's what brings us satisfaction. Millennials, on the other hand, have a view of more profound teamwork where simultaneous work occurs and technology plays the largest role. Thus job descriptions, interview questions, methods of assessments, and even how our psychometric tests that were originally designed by us are all out of date!

What do we trust? What tools do we use if people who designed these behavoural theory-based tools all come from an age where digital technology was not the main driver for work behaviour, and where sentiments and characteristics of humans differed? I am convinced that the only thing that cannot be produced by science, artificial intelligence, and technology is people's consciousness. This is why I seek to know the person as a human being even if the interviewees find the questions mundane and boring, I seek to find out who they are outside of the technical domain.

When recruiting, our generation of Xers value authority, autonomy, and job security. Our loyalty towards our bosses and work is paramount, so knowledge and clarity on that during this phase of recruitment is vital. Thinking of these a necessity, we describe them in our interviews to millennials who don't care about oak docrs and fancy facades, but rather want a bean bag, a laptop, and unlimited WIFI. They look for purpose in their toil and where the learning and growth is. They have been wired differently. Millennials expect to receive information about work environment, communication patterns/modes, and structures. They expect flexibility in timings and an appreciation of overall performance. They want suggestions, schemes, and new idea-generation channels rather than policies and procedures and the rigid structures we offer them with explanations of the scales within each band.

When recruiting millennials, we must be equipped, and take this task from the top by bringing the latest techniques into play. We should introduce video applications instead of looking at traditional CVs. We must travel at optimal speed in order to cope with this internet-born generation. A survey shows that 89% of jobseekers are likely to use a mobile device to find work in the next year since 80% of young adults between the ages of 18-34 own a smartphone. But on the other hand, 87% of companies are not investing adequately in mobile-friendly recruitment. During interviews, we must remember to put emphasis on culture since our company brands are our ambassadors in a transparent world like this. Engagement starts before hiring, so inviting potential hires to spend time with real employees or android/virtual worlds will feed millennials' keenness to know why they should take this job beyond the paycheck.

It is evident that the differences between generations is influenced by changes due to experience, life phases, and career stages. The simple fact that each generation entered the work world at differing points in time suggests that there are definite differences that exist between generations.

"With millennials, every gadget imaginable is almost an extension of their bodies. they multitask, talk, walk, listen and type and detect. and their priorities are simple; they come first!" — **MORLEY SAFER**

There are several approaches to classifying work values—the most common being used to distinguish between work values that are extrinsic or intrinsic. A survey by Deloitte has found that millennials wanted businesses to focus more on "people and purpose." It is not surprising, in light of this fact, that many studies on millennials, particularly those on workforce patterns, focus on concerns that millennials may be following radically different career trajectories than prior generations.

Gen Y Speaking

Lots of labels have been used to describe my generation. By some, we are even referred to as the "me-generation"—just another way to convey narcissism at its highest levels. And I am not here to argue about stereotypes because why bother? My job is to convey the other side of the coin—the fact that our generation is more tech-savvy, more in number, better educated, and more diverse in most aspects. Our social habits are different—the good kind of different. We enormously value teamwork, modesty and good conduct.

Millennials corner the market in tech prowess. We grew up with WiFi, smartphones, laptops and social media at our disposal. We have unprecedented access to information. Our affinity for the digital world and greater connectivity is what distinguishes us from previous generations, and we can clearly witness how that has substantially manifested its way into the workplace. Forty-one percent of millennials are reported to have stated that they prefer to resort to electronic communication with their peers at work, rather than discuss matters over the phone or face-to-face (PWC Opinion Research, 2011). But then again, who wouldn't agree that technology makes us more effective at work?

But the greatest difference of all lies in what we perceive we can get from the workplace. What essentially influences our career decision is its alignment with our values and personal goals. We often engage in community service and we expect more opportunities for social responsibility from our employers. It might sound surprising to some, but monetary perks are not at the forefront of our checklists. In fact, the environment and culture is far more essential. We appreciate a fun working environment. We give greater value to non-monetary perks that serve us in achieving a work-life balance—such as flexible working hours— and essentially, a culture that nurtures teamwork with emphasis on belonging and acceptance.

If we were to compare our generation to our predecessors—Gen X—we are far more optimistic about our success and our future. Gen

X does not expect to find self-fulfillment in their careers. They look for it outside of their jobs. We, on the other hand, have higher expectations with regards to success. We thrive wherever we feel worthy and of value—wherever we are given the chance to contribute and are able to innovate.

It is apparent that a workplace can benefit tremendously from a better understanding of the differences in core values, ideologies, and thinking patterns, depending on the generation. The technological and digital revolutions of today are unlike anything that the first revolutions of steam power, electric power, mass production, electronics and even IT and automation were. Gen Y is somewhat a product of the technological age, thus able to thrive in this fast-changing environment where labour markets are shifting because of the fusion of technologies. Automation has already begun displacing the basic manual skilled workforce. Social stability is already under threat due to artificial intelligence and its capacity to replace human jobs and minds. One third of the world's population is already using social media platforms to connect, learn, and share information. The big question is: what will Gen X do to adapt and ensure they are not made redundant?

It is with all this in mind that companies should consider breaking down the hierarchical structures that have conventionally kept younger and less-experienced employees from having a greater voice within organisations. Companies which will continue to excel are those that recognise the invaluable talent that millennials can bring to

"The millennial generation will entirely recast the image of youth from downbeat and alienated to upbeat and engaged..."— **NEIL HOWE AND WILLIAM STRAUSS**

the table in order to assist companies with the transition into this digital age. The ability of companies to adapt will determine their survival.

If there is one thing that we all agree on, despite the generational gap, is the fact that technology has completely transformed the way we do things. Our needs and demands as individuals and as a society has grown and changed altogether. But the most inevitable change of all is that of mindsets. New ideologies need to evolve—businesses cannot simply run the way they used to.

THE COMPROMISE
FROM A MILLENNIAL – GEN Y

"As a recent graduate, I have been waiting all my life to finally gain independence and to finally start taking the first steps in my career journey. But as I stand here, done with the first step of many, I feel uncomfortable about entering a world that is so rigid in its corporate structures, and one that is yet to break free from information silos.

The thing about workers in general is that we compromise our own goals and personal values. However, having a fulfilling job is at the top of our checklist when we are seeking a career.

The need to be happy is the top most consideration when making our lifestyle and career choices. That is why 'playbour' (work that feels like leisure) is crucial in firing up our commitment levels.

Passion for the job is one thing we millennials will not be willing to sabotage or renege on. Even if the pay is mediocre, I would rather do something I love than have a high-paid job that doesn't get me out of bed in the morning.

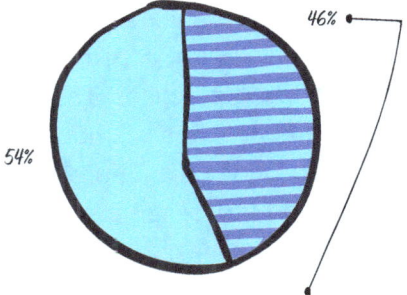

IN THE MIDDLE EAST

46% of entrepreneurs started their businesses at school or university, the highest proportion of any country or region in the world.

SOURCE: Entrepreneurial Creatives, Skeptical – The Truth about MENA Millennials, Chayme Samir, World Economic Forum, 2017

The reality is that the current economic conditions have forced many of us to compromise when taking up a job. Seventy-two percent of youth surveyed stated that they have settled (traded-off) in some way to get work. Thirty-eight percent of those who are currently working said that they were actively seeking other work. On the other hand, another study has shown that 70% of millennials said that civil engagement is amongst their highest priorities; therefore, being part of organisations that contribute to the society is desirable."

BRIDGING WORKPLACE
GENERATIONAL GAPS – GEN X

A lthough differences exist, it is also important to note that these generalised views should not be used as stereotyping mechanisms. Millennials want to be able to work in the way that suits them best. Their prominent use of technology means that the line between work and home life has become increasingly blurred, although many would prefer to work in an office environment rather than in a solitary one such as at home. It is also true that while Gen Y values diversity and typically seeks out employers with strong equality and a strong approach to their operations, their expectations are not always met in practice.

Millennials feel constrained by what they see as outdated, traditional working practices. They feel that rigid hierarchies and outdated management styles will not succeed in getting the most out of them. Most are under the impression that their managers do not always understand the best, most effective or efficient use of technology in the workplace. A huge majority believe that merit should be based on outcomes, not time spent executing. There is a growing trend now where you find offices becoming meeting spaces rather than fixed working locations.

We must attract bright millennial minds into the established workplace. Millennials desire to learn and progress, and this directly impacts their views on benefits that employers offer. Most Gen Y employees prefer training and development and flexible working opportunities over financial benefits. This doesn't mean they don't have standards on pay and working conditions that they prefer, but purposeful careers would be of much higher priority to their employment agenda.

It is so important then, for companies to implement workplace solutions that will accommodate the conflicting views and needs of a diverse workforce—from the baby boomer generation to Generation X to millennials. It is certainly a challenge, but if not addressed, these will negatively impact the potential of companies to survive in a highly competitive global space which requires companies to invest more and more in the retention of top talent.

The intergenerational tensions that usually appear can often be explained by a lack of understanding between generations. When Generation Xers stop thinking that Gen Y employees have an unreasonable sense of entitlement, and millennials begin to exercise some patience and offer help in assisting with the transition into more respon-

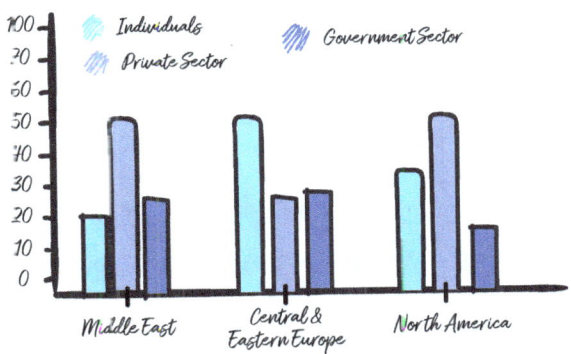

DOES PRIVATE SECTOR HAVE INFLUENCE?

42% said the private sector has the strongest influence, while 27% chose the government. Individuals alone were seen as having less ability to influence society. When it comes to influencing an organization, however, only a quarter of millennials in the Middle East chose it as a goal, in comparison to nearly half in Europe and North America.

SOURCE: We are More Different than You Think, Instead, Emerging Markets Institue, The Head Foundation and Universum, 2018

sive organisational structures, things will improve.

In an effort to help managers put themselves in younger employees' shoes and to coach senior executives in IT, social media, and the latest workplace trends, many organisations are beginning to pair top management with younger employees in programmes referred to as 'reverse mentoring'. Such initiatives are also meant to help in the transferring of corporate knowledge to millennials, which will become increasingly important as the older generation starts to enter retirement.

TIPS WORTHY OF CONSIDERATION:

#1 When hiring millennials discuss their personal aspirations and always structure your packages with a dose of offerings that truly promote work/life balance.

#2 While interviewing, ensure that you reflect a deeper understanding of diversity and gender equality, and discuss it.

#3 Talk about technology and show them that Gen Xers are capable and adaptable and, in fact, "connected" and Net-literate like they are.

#4 In your HR policies and decisions, help millennials and Gen Xers alike grow in the workplace by eliminating age discrimination and creating different channels of growth and development for each track, compatible with their learning preferences.

#5 As hard as it is to let go of the organisational practices that made Gen Xers who they are today in policies and codes of conduct, they need to loosen their tight grip and give millennials more flexibility. At the end, it's the purpose (the "why") of working that will make them produce higher results... and not the "What or "How".

Chapter Two

NAVIGATING THE WORKPLACE

Mrs. Hope

"Keeping these overzealous millennials grounded may be a daunting task in the face of managers from my generation who were inducted into the workforce with the swim-or-sink welcome pack rather than the handholding that Generation Y feels entitled to. I'm concerned that these new on-boarding techniques will not effectively build the grit and resilience required to grow. Our generation didn't receive any type of special treatment, nor did we see the need for it.

The demonstration of responsibility expected of us allowed us to forge our way up the corporate ladder based on our own personal development., and that's why I worry that these millennials will not develop the personal initiative and leadership 'smarts' that are essential for achieving success. But I have to acknowledge the inevitable fact that millennials are dominating the workforce and expect defined goals, engagement and transparency. In order to accommodate Gen Y and seamlessly integrate them into the existing workplace frameworks, I will require greater flexibility from my management. We will be faced with changing the way we operate in order to foster an atmosphere of belonging which millennials seem to value. Or else, how will we be able to retain them?

Now that we have managed to achieve our insourcing targets, how do I manage to convince our HR that these millennials will not be easy to retain? These traditional induction packs will unlikely keep them engaged! For many, getting onboard will mean clarifying roles and responsibilities and getting to know their way around an organisation. For millennials, it is about establishing a foundation within the business and learning about the company's history. How we manage this onboarding process will be what differentiates us from other traditional organizations, so we can solidify workplace loyalty from day one. The first few weeks of a millennial's employment largely determines their career trajectory with the company. There is no doubt that creative onboarding will take time and effort to implement, but how else can we manage to captivate their interests and capture their attention?

I will have to propose to the GM tomorrow and convince him that I need him to tell his story. Storytelling and building the company's persona in the minds of these new millennia recruits is essential. They must meet him, feel his spirit and know about the company's vision from him directly. This will surely enthuse them. It is strange how simple communication makes a big difference to the clarity that they need going forward. They not only need the 'whats' answered like my generation, but they need to hear the 'whys'.

Saj

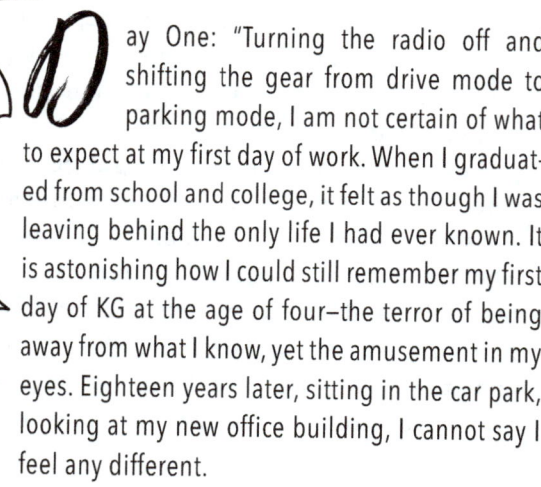

ay One: "Turning the radio off and shifting the gear from drive mode to parking mode, I am not certain of what to expect at my first day of work. When I graduated from school and college, it felt as though I was leaving behind the only life I had ever known. It is astonishing how I could still remember my first day of KG at the age of four—the terror of being away from what I know, yet the amusement in my eyes. Eighteen years later, sitting in the car park, looking at my new office building, I cannot say I feel any different.

As I leave my car I realize that life is expanding, and college notes are a part of yesterday. There is no turning back now—that's for sure. Approaching the elevator, I cannot help but feel disoriented, not knowing whether I will feel welcomed in an environment filled with the older crowd, especially since most of them think that we have an unsustainable sense of entitlement!

Being escorted to our cubicles (myself and a bunch of other young new recruits), I feel a little less apprehensive. People around us seem friendly. We are invited to join them for breakfast. I am not sure if this is their idea of an orientation, but I am curious to see what they have in store for us."

Day Five: "It is the last day of the week (Thursday)—the semi-formal day. I feel much more at ease wearing a pair of jeans, comfortable sneakers, and simply, looking my age. The team and I won't be meeting clients today; neither do our roles require us to be at a front desk. For back-office support, this should be how we dress daily, but making such a request would be ridiculed and deemed as simply wanting to be fun, social, and laid-back at the expense of being productive. I remember once reading an MTV-sponsored study during school days, stating that 88% of millennials want to be friends with their co-workers, 81% want to make their own hours, and 79% want to wear jeans to work. It baffled me back then, but it does not sound far off from reality today.

This terrible cliché and sweeping stereotype that has been the talk of the season as my generation auditions its way into the labour market makes us wonder—what if that same amount of energy was invested into altering the workplace culture and adapting pragmatic solutions that would promote a balanced perspective for the two generations? Current workplace models fail to attract, engage and retain modern talent and are if anything, outdated.

We grew up in a fully digitalized world. Our behaviour is rooted in our upbringing, and it will continue having a greater impact in the generations following us. Thus, if businesses began to accept the fact that technology is taking over our everyday lives and has changed the way we get things done, then it is imperative to embrace the thought of integrating modern behaviours in order to create an engaging and profitable organisation.

An hour was left for finishing the day and the atmosphere was casual, given that we were about to kick-start the weekend. So I decided to walk around and meet people who I hadn't had the chance to speak to earlier in the week. There she was. I could hear her voice and feel her energy from across the corridor. I've idolised her for years and always tried to put on a positive front around her. My intuition tells me that I can openly talk to her. She would surely understand. She is unlike any Gen Xer I know. Sugarcoating is not part of her language, and needless to say, I need none.

Her glance met mine, and she hesitantly asked me about my first few days."

GENERATION Y IS DRIVING AN
UNPRECEDENTED WORK-LIFE CULTURE SHIFT

E very generation develops a set of values that drives attitudes and ideas about work, and Generation Y is no exception. As tomorrow's leaders, millennials are prioritising creativity to work and in finding meaning in what they do. Although the interaction between generations can seem as a seedbed for tension and conflict, as a matter of fact, in most instances, it actually results in a transformation often referred to as the "cohort effect".

Without a doubt, millennials are the largest, most educated, and most diverse generation to enter the workforce. Comprising a little more than half of the working population, millennials enter the labour-market with a different learning style, comfort-level with technology, expectations of work-life balance, and different ways of relating to managers and peers. Thus, on-boarding techniques, training and development, and retention become of paramount importance and a challenge facing organisations today. Leveraging social learning, mobile technology and micro-learning to meet the needs of millennials is the basis of such effective onboarding. This not only impacts hard factors such as productivity, retention, and turnover costs but also soft factors such as employer reputation, corporate culture, engagement and referrals for open positions.

Recruiting and onboarding are important functions for attracting millennials into the workplace, which is why leaders are vital when it comes to retention of millennial staff. They tend to have the greatest amount of responsibility and influence when delegating and making daily interactions with millennials.

Millennials are driven by a unique combination of ambition for career progression, a personal mission, and a desire for continuous growth and learning. A Microsoft survey shows that 88% of millennials are drawn to companies that display strong and clear values. Six in ten millennials say that "a sense of purpose" is the reason why they chose an employer. This is a signal that *story* matters. In today's organisations, telling a compelling story that is representative of the brand is crucial. The motivation to creating such strong stories is often pushed to the backburner due to priorities being focused on meeting targets—to the detriment of some companies as far as appealing to millennials goes. To the older generations of baby boomers, loyalty to organisations was not tied so much to development opportunities. However, even Generation X and Y managers are more likely to be loyal and stay with a company if care is taken to develop them as leaders.

Millennials seek employers that invest in training and development and regularly present opportunities while demonstrating pathways for long-term progression. Time is of the essence because optimal productivity takes time. Research shows that it takes 18-22 weeks for professionals and 24-28 weeks for executives to reach full productivity. Effective onboarding can reduce the learning curve and make employees more productive faster.

> "Instead of complaining about adapting for millennials, it's imperative for leaders and managers to acknowledge the role of millennial behavior as an indication of the needs of the modern workplace to attract, leverage, and retain modern talent."
> — CRYSTAL KADAKIA, The Millennial Myth: Transforming Misunderstanding Into Workplace Breakthroughs

Millennials also prefer their training to be multi-dimensional, which offers them an array of work-styles and opportunities in accordance with a dynamic and futuristic approach to the business. When these two factors—career development and on-the-job learning are combined, millennials tend to stick around.

According to Price Waterhouse Cooper's "Millennials at Work - Reshaping the Workplace" study, career progression is a top priority for millennials, with 52% reporting that this element alone is what draws them to particular employers over others. Another study shows that 65% of millennials who had recently accepted jobs said the opportunity for personal development was the factor that most influenced their decision.

THE FACTS

Fifty-eight percent of millennials are said to expect to leave their jobs within three years, according to the 2015 Millennial Workforce, 2014 Elance Desk survey. Only 16% of millennials think they will be with their current employers in ten years,as reported by the 2016 Deloitte Millennial Survey, "Winning over the next generation of leaders 2016". It is no wonder then that 53% of hiring managers say that it is difficult to find and recruit millennial employees. Another study by PWC shows that 65% of millennials who had recently accepted jobs said that the opportunity for personal development was the factor that most influenced their decision.

The role of technology in recruitment serves as a benefit to the potential employee and a resource to the employer. By using the Internet, in particular, social networking websites open up possibilities for better recruitment while providing valuable information about worthwhile talent in the workforce. Generation Y is marked by having a strong profound communications and technological impact through the use of computers, social media, cellphones, and other digital technology products.

To effectively address the workforce demand, companies ought to understand Generation Y's characteristics and factors that influence their work attitudes. This will help them with recruitment and retention efforts. It's important for prospective employees to make use of social platforms to allow easy access to information about potential employers, but it's even more important for employers to be in tune with the millennial mentality.

Development opportunities really matter to young employees and next generation managers. Work-life flexibility is crucial and this generation is much more upfront about voicing these issues. In terms of learning, this generation has low boredom thresholds and is more willing to embrace virtual learning and learning with peers. Organisations need to find ways to engage millennials in a manner that they find compelling and consistent with their distinct values and tremendous ambition.

WHAT MILLENNIALS REPORT AS TOP PRIORITIES WHEN CONSIDERING AN EMPLOYER

Millennial survey respondents rated as very important.

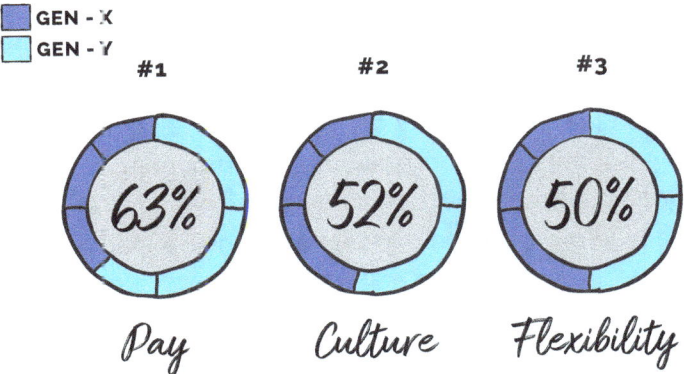

GEN - X
GEN - Y

#1 #2 #3

63% 52% 50%

Pay Culture Flexibility

GOOD PAY AND POSITIVE CULTURES ATTRACT MILLENNIALS AND GEN Z, BUT DIVERSITY/INCLUSION AND FLEXIBILITY ARE IMPORTANT KEYS TO KEEPING THEM HAPPY

Percentage of millennials saying they will stay beyond five years:

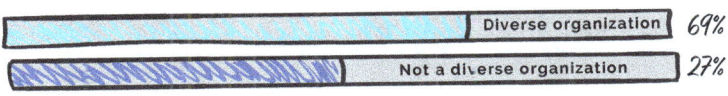

Diverse organization 69%

Not a diverse organization 27%

55% of millennials who say their organizations are more flexible compared to three years ago plan to stay at least five years. Where they see less flexibility, only 17 percent plan to stay long-term

SOURCE: Delloitte Millennial Survey 2018

The importance of catering to the millennial generation is being recognized more and more on a global scale. In times of increasing complexity, mobility, and speed of change, many businesses and organisations cannot afford to rely on the current mechanisms of selection for their leadership talent, but need to put additional effort into developing these skills. Organisations that create an active learning culture will benefit from increased loyalty and commitment of their younger workers and therefore have the advantage of higher retention and talent sustainability.

Gen Y Speaking

As millennials, our priorities are a bit different from those of previous generations. We value innovation and want our ideas to be heard. We also prefer to quickly complete projects, not simply getting through work hours. Second-guessing our superiors' expectations is never a good thing, so we would rather have clear directions and regular feedback in order to improve and also ensure that we are on the right track. Mentorship is also something us Gen Y employees value, particularly in an up-or-out culture where an ethos of "survival of the fittest" and natural selection dominate and altruism is out of the picture. It would be nice to have more interaction and guidance from senior employees. We believe this type of arrangement would be mutually beneficial and good for business overall. Knowing how our individual tasks impact and support the company's overarching goals is a great motivator for us millennials. We don't want to feel like mere machines on a production line. We desire a greater understanding of the value we bring and expect companies to reward us for our hard work.

Gen X Speaking

It is obvious that the challenges facing us are ones that have to do with acceptance of something different. We seek the basics of empathy, appreciation, value, respect for authority and other such principles which have been instilled in our very being by our parents and educators. The battle that exists between millennials and us starts from school with teachers today complaining about these new minds whose expectations are skyrocketing while they don't give back the basics we expect. This dilemma may seem a daunting task to overcome, but I shall be positive and try to simplify it in order to solve it. Accepting that we are just different is the first step. Not judging who is right and who is wrong is even more basic as a first promise to the solutions that are ahead.

Millennials are not looking to fill a slot in a faceless company any more than a good venture capitalist is looking to toss money at a faceless startup. They're looking strategically at opportunities to invest their time and energy in a place where they can make a difference, preferably a place that itself makes a difference. It would help to find ways to coach them to be better employees; as millennials need to be told the expectations of organisations in a way that makes sense to them. That is something I shall surely try to educate all my managers about so that I pave the way for a bridge that is much needed.

THE COMPROMISE: POSSIBLE SOLUTIONS

While millennials prefer the flexibility to work outside the office, they are also comfortable in group settings. They prefer to work as part of a team in order to accomplish independent tasks as they use the skills, knowledge, and resources of team members to satisfy individual needs. But when it comes to interaction with manage-

MORE DISMAY BY MILLENNIALS OF THE CORPORATE WORLD

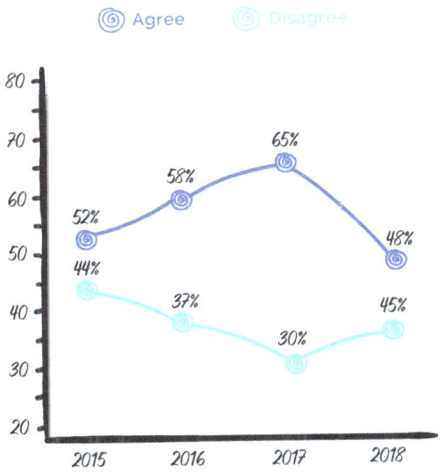

Corporates behave in an ethical manner

SOURCE Deloitte Millennial Survey 2018

ment, Generation Y feels more valued if managers work with them on an individual level. This is a point that managers need to take into consideration if they hope to win the loyalty of millennials

Workplace attitudes which motivate and guide millennials' career paths include flexibility, team orientation, individualism and continual learning. In order for companies to effectively attract and retain top talent, they need to adapt recruitment strategies in a way that addresses characteristics and attitudes of Generation Y employees. As an example, as most millennials desire greater flexibility, employers should aim to provide opportunities for an adequate work-life balance in addition to providing flexible schedules and benefit plans.

CORPORATE WORLD CARES ABOUT MONEY

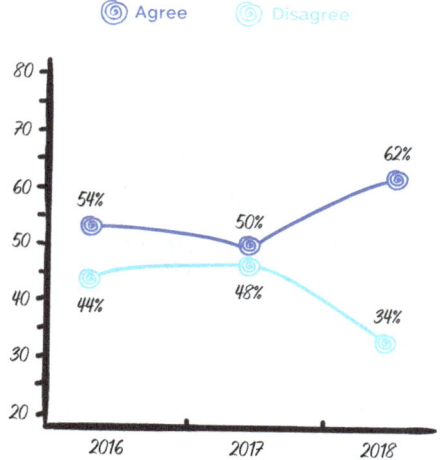

Corporates have no ambition beyond wanting to make money

SOURCE: Deloitte Millennial Survey 2018

Since millennials actually have much in common with their older colleagues, understanding who they are and what they value in a workplace offers several benefits for companies. It helps companies attract, integrate, and retain these techy, social-media-savvy workers and also provides insight into how to improve their organisations to benefit employees of all ages.

Employers and managers of millennials have to be tech-savvy and have to learn to communicate with Gen Y in the language they understand best. For example, texting could be more effective than emails, so incorporating this could help bridge a gap. Some responsive organisations have already started creating their own internal social network sites that allow them to connect with others in an informal basis on a platform that is not policed. This way they can share their status updates on a constant basis as they go through the ups and downs of their work day.

On the other hand, up against an unfortunate professional reputation, millennials must actively prove themselves to their employers and older co-workers. It's important for them to remain flexible, hardworking, and patient. While many hope to find a fast-track to career advancement, adjusting to a new workplace and building a career takes time.

Keeping the driving values of the Gen Y in mind, HR teams can adapt to these millennials and leverage on their strengths. Providing an atmosphere where millennials can thrive will lead to greater retention rates, and understanding how millennials gather and digest information will also assist employers in recruitment. The Gen Y learner's requirements and expectations of the learning environment are different from boomers and Gen Xers. That's why it's imperative for companies to redesign training and development programmes to make them more inclusive and accommodate the differences of the millennial generation.

TIPS WORTHY OF CONSIDERATION:

#1 Millennials simply want to be heard at work and feel like their ideas matter. They want to express their ideas, but that doesn't imply that they expect their manager will always agree with them or accept their ideas. What they distaste is being dismissed as being too naive or inexperienced to have valuable opinions.

#2 Some possible actions you could take to help keep the Gen Y interested may include creating online and social experiences for them. Training and onboarding programmes must look at content, structure, and delivery methods. The methods of learning can include bite-sized videos and information for micro-learning delivered in an ongoing manner over longer periods of time.

#3 Millennials crave social feedback and mentoring. It increases their engagement. Xers complain that coaching takes time, but through micro-coaching, this can be conducted throughout the day via their mobile devices. For instance, training tips can be sent by WhatsApp, companies can connect via Snapchat to train and use innovative and current ways of knowledge transmission. This increased frequency will help in building rapport and trust faster and creating enhanced engagement and loyalty.

#4 Other considerations that companies should make include enabling on-site child care, subsidized off-site child care, emergency child care, flexi-place, job sharing, personal day plans, and flexi-time.

Chapter Three
THAT MAKE-OR-BREAK ANNUAL EVENT

Mrs. Hope

"We are in the midst of one of the greatest debates the talent management field has ever seen. And what is the pressing topic? Performance management! It's that time of the year to hold performance reviews and with all these new recruits, I am expecting all hell to break loose. I am honestly wondering what I should do. I must convince the boss to take all the managers on a weekend of intensive training. We must be prepared to meet the expectations of these millennials that are all anxiously waiting ever-more-so prepared than we were or will be.

We all expect feedback on a more regular basis, and I have been alluding to that for years now. There is a marked difference from our generation who simply view managerial attention as a type of performance improvement plan. The millennial mindset is to put oneself out there and try an activity, gather feedback about how to do better, and use the goal of getting to the next step as motivation for performance improvement. For the most part, since childhood, millennials have functioned in an environment that encourages both feedback for improvement and an open structure to promote advancement. Frequent feedback is what is expected. This environment is their playbook for winning and should be *ours*! But, where is the metric? Where is the objective fairness? Imagine a world in which manager/employee relationships thrive on mentorship and coaching. Imagine annual reviews going completely extinct. Wouldn't managers have greater influence on, and more meaningful relationships with their employees? It would result in a lot of team building, and thus less competition. Employee tensions will therefore subside through increased dialogue. This is what Gen Y thrives on— and more so Gen-Z who will be creeping in sooner than we think.

> *"Performance management as practiced by most organizations has become a rule-based, bureaucratic process, existing as an end in itself rather than actually shaping performance. Employees hate it. Managers hate it. Even HR departments hate it."* — LASZLO BOCK

I'm trying to find a way of reducing the need for the quantitative performance review report and instilling the practice of ongoing feedback in this organisation through a major coaching/training initiative, when my favourite millennial arrives and knocks on my door. I instantly feel uneasy because I know as a company we have not developed up-to-date performance management systems that millennials like Saj will find satisfactory. Businesses that wish to boost millennial engagement and reap the vast benefits these workers can bring, should think about how they currently assess and review employees. Taking a well-devised, competency-based approach that effectively blends career development, performance and employee aspirations could really help strengthen an organisation and give it market advantage.

My workforce is changing and the old processes our HR have relied on for the past generations simply won't be effective today. We must adjust our performance measurement and feedback systems to meet the demands of our new team."

Saj

"I am mentally absent while preparing breakfast with my colleagues in the kitchen, unsure of what to expect from my manager during my performance appraisal later this afternoon. I hate being uncertain-who would not anyway? I do know the standard of work I have delivered this entire year was up to mark. I know the impact of the projects I have worked on. What I do not know is how *pleased* my manager is with the quality of my work and how he will be measuring my KPIs?

Looking back at the multiple milestones accomplished—most of which were completed prior to their set deadlines—I do not recall ever sitting one-to-one and receiving feedback on my performance. Frankly, I am not even sure if my manager appreciates me getting the work done sooner than anticipated or whether or not he prefers receiving tasks right at their deadline. All I ever get in response is an astounding facial expression that I find hard to decode.

I was lost in my thoughts, trying to envision the rundown, but the scenarios could go either way. We did not set expectations at the beginning of the year and that stretches the gap even wider. I was hoping for an open dialogue—one that would help me grow and develop. I suddenly smell something burning—my toast is no longer edible. My skeptical mind can't help but take this as a sign.

Walking out of the kitchen, I pray that I don't leave the performance review meeting blinds ded. A glimpse of hope was suddenly walking my way. There she was, the on y manager I could confide in."

A new generation of employees requires a new set of performance management policies.

Performance reviews are "a curse on corporate America" according to UCLA researcher Samuel Culberts. Research psychologists at Kansas State University, Eastern Kentucky University, and Texas A&M recently examined the effect of negative feedback during annual performance reviews which led to lack of motivation for improvement and even positive comments being misconstrued. Performance reviews typically classify people as "exceeding expectations," "meeting expectations," or "not meeting expectations." According to Dr. David Rock of the NeuroLeadership Institute, being categorized triggers a fight-or-flight reaction in people which in turn can interfere with the impact of the feedback being given—even if it is positive.

Millennials think differently because they have grown up influenced heavily by rapid advancements in technology. Therefore, it is essential that forward-thinking companies adapt their performance review processes to better suit the Gen Y's way of thinking.

In order to achieve high performance, employee engagement is an important factor to put into consideration. In essence, performance monitoring procedures ought to be designed in a way that improves employee engagement and addresses the new work habits (including the use of technology) while also being easy to use and visually attractive.

> "With more and more millennials navigating their way into the corporate world, hierarchies have to disappear. Millennials value an environment of mutual interest and passion. Thus, talent management strategies will have to be reformed to "look more like Facebook, and less like pyramid structures"— VINEET NAYAR

The purpose of a performance management system should be to provide the business intelligence that enables an enterprise to make the right decisions in real time. Information portals capturing work data now is analysed so extensively that it provides managers with views and conclusions that can drive daily and timely feedback given to employees. However, when looking into the current standard of performance management and reviews, there is clear disconnect with the requirements of today's world of work that is populated by so many millennials.

The process of performance appraisals should ideally be reinvented so that "people management" administrative systems and technologies meet the expectations of Gen Y. By adopting regular and flexible reporting that is simplified and instantly accessible companies can execute effective performance appraisals.

Millennials are team players, feedback seekers, top performers, and job hoppers with differences in their work style which will change the way performance reviews ought to be conducted in today's businesses. When Gen Y discusses performance reviews and recognition for a job well done, they are not talking about ranking systems but rather about nurturing ongoing relationships between employers and employees. From a millennial's perspective, that is one of the ways companies can gain their loyalty.

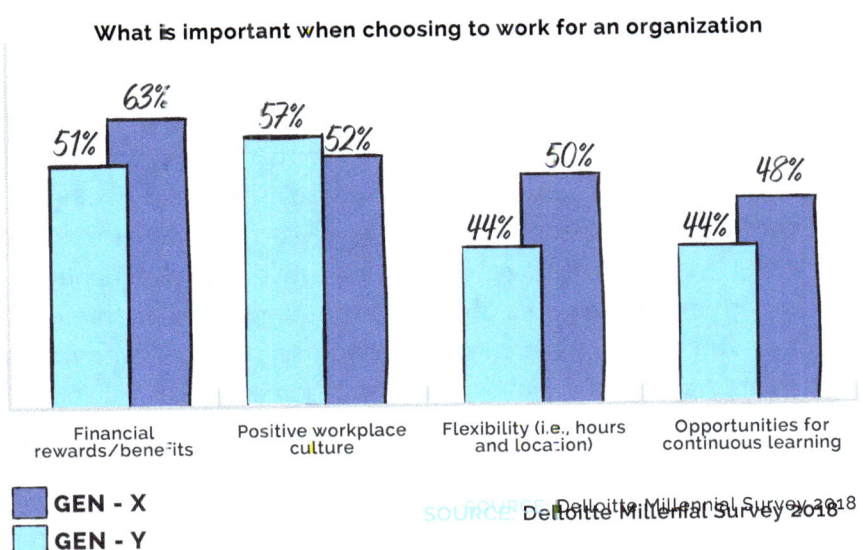

**PAY AND POSITIVE WORKPLACE CULTURE
— TOP YOUNG WORKERS' WISHLIST**

What is important when choosing to work for an organization

- 63%
- 51%
- 57%
- 52%
- 50%
- 44%
- 48%
- 44%

Financial rewards/benefits | Positive workplace culture | Flexibility (i.e., hours and location) | Opportunities for continuous learning

GEN - X
GEN - Y

SOURCE: Deloitte Millennial Survey 2018

Conventional performance reviews which revolve around measuring an employee's achievements against a set list of objectives in an appraisal meeting are simply irrelevant to the millennial generation workforce. While most employees don't like performance reviews, the millennial generation in particular resent them even more. Most Gen Y workers believe that the performance review process needs an upgrade, if not a complete overhaul. Companies need to realize that poor performance reviews can put off potentially good employees. Having a quality performance review process that includes frequent, relevant feedback is a top driver of engagement for millennials. Studies show that a significant majority of businesses still rely on spreadsheets to track their performance metrics instead of adopting technologies that can help gather feedback faster and easier and provide employees with transparency while creating greater engagement and better retention.

There are many issues that contribute to the attitude millennials have towards management when it comes to performance review procedures. Many millennials view annual reviews as simply archaic administration procedures that companies feel obliged to conduct just to meet their operational regulatory requirements, rather than an actual attempt to appraise workers' performance and productivity standards. The reason for this is that the lack of consistent feedback throughout the year cannot be compensated for with one review at the end of the year. Gen Y employees constantly raise the issue of feeling that they are left in the dark regarding their performance levels, which then makes year-end reviews a daunting prospect.

Also, the fact that standard annual performance reviews take longer means that millennials prefer shorter feedback sessions. The other major problem with traditional performance reviews is that they focus on the individual's performance over the entire past year. Consequently, traditional performance reviews fail to provide employees with immediate feedback on how they are currently performing. This delayed response contributes to the loss of interest and engagement, especially of millennial employees who are accustomed to receiving instant feedback on social media.

Another complaint millennials often raise is the issue of vague performance reviews. Because most managers tend to use generic performance guidance sheets, Gen Y feels that the reviews are not personalized enough to accurately assess their value. Managers and employers should consider making their feedback specific and measurable as this will help employees improve their performance. Thus, companies need to radically change their processes for sharing feedback in order to retain top talent and stay competitive.

Employees don't need annual performance reviews to know how they stack up against their peers. Companies need to stop merely *managing* performance and actually start *developing* it. While goal achievement shouldn't be the *only* metric for measuring performance, setting regular, smaller-scale goals for employees can give managers a way to offer real-time, agile feedback that actually works.

Gen X Speaking

Workers need to understand the corporate culture and the most effective communication style within their workplace in order to show their strengths more effectively.

In an increasingly digital workforce, annual performance measures feel outmoded and disengaging with little regard to the needs of the growing millennial population. Therefore, it's time for managers to revise their review practices. There are reasons why most annual performance reviews are not effective in motivating millennials to improve their performance. One of these reasons includes the fact that reviews are done infrequently. Supervisors and employees look at performance plans once or twice a year and by the next review, the large majority have forgotten what their goals were. Also, behaviours are usually tied to the supervisor's goals and not to organisational values or to the company mission, so goals tend to change with changes in management. This review and reward system thus becomes delayed and defunct.

Gen Y is often overwhelmed when they enter the workforce because of the Reviews structures in the business world. Unless performance reviews address their individual strengths and discuss how their current position and performance will affect their personal goals, the feedback won't feel relevant.

Gen Y Speaking

Millennials are used to feedback, and lots of it. Nearly half of all working millennials want to be recognized at least monthly for the good work that they are doing. This proves that the current once or twice a year reviews conducted by employers simply do not suffice. Setting up a one-on-one monthly meeting to recognize their efforts and giving them an opportunity to raise their concerns will drastically reduce the dissatisfaction levels in the workplace that are largely caused by this lack of regular communication with regards to performance monitoring.

Feedback must always be pursued. Growing up, Generation Y always sought that motivation from their surroundings. At home, our siblings would do whatever it takes to earn our parents' approval. At school, we would push ourselves to work hard just to be recognized by teachers. The equation was simple and straightforward. All we had to do was excel in something, then get praised for it, thus resulting in feeling motivated to deliver more and keeping the energy level consistent. And all good things would prevail. Though outdated, this perspective feels very relevant to how feedback systems are formulated in some current company cultures.

Gen X say we display an abundance of self-confidence as we claim to be the "can do" generation. We millennials believe that we are an asset to the organisation from the get-go. So the bar being set too high is our own doing. We always strive to set new challenges to achieve, to take on new job skills, and we always seem to discount failure from the equation. However, I would be lying if I said that we are not cautious. Having to graduate at a time of a financial crisis and looking for employment during an economic downturn only increases the likelihood of us pursuing self-employment and focusing on developing ourselves for the sake of merely surviving without being too reliant on a particular job. It is evident that we do not value corporate loyalty, as we do not perceive it to be a source of reward nor of job security.

Companies should think of creating a personalized suite of benefits that offers more flexibility and choice to better meet the needs of a diverse workforce. This can be done through the introduction of enhanced performance management systems that include creative ways of assessment and providing ongoing feedback which could be highly beneficial to employees.

Companies must address the needs of their millennial employees' ongoing performance with and real-time feedback delivered in a coaching-like fashion capacity. Managers can communicate in real time with constructive insights and ensure that feedback is connected to current goals and projects. Remember, millennials are interested in the *why*. Simply instructing them on what needs to be done is not good enough. They want a "no- fuss working environment" that is clear about the reasons behind set objectives. They are not interested in doing meaningless work just to keep themselves occupied. They have a strong desire to know that their contributions matter and are in fact influencing a positive change and impact on whatever they do.

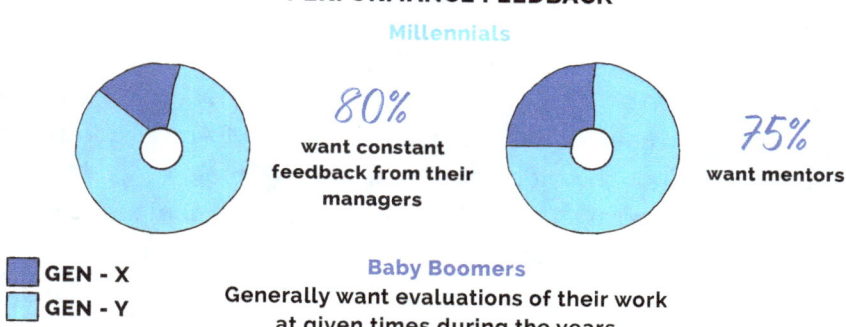

PERFORMANCE FEEDBACK

Millennials

80%

want constant feedback from their managers

75%

want mentors

■ **GEN - X**
□ **GEN - Y**

Baby Boomers
Generally want evaluations of their work at given times during the years

SOURCE: Future Workplaces' Multiple Generations @ Work Survey, 2013

Benchmarking your company against others is essential because there is a lot to learn a lot from that process and you can then ensure that you are doing your best in synthesising the best solutions that suit you. IBM has developed internal tools that encourage a feedback culture by allowing employees within to provide their anonymous reviews across all levels of staff in the business. Adobe replaced annual reviews with frequent bi-monthly check-ins that strive to keep the lines of communication between staff and employers open. These types of performance reviews would ultimately help to create more dynamic pathways for leadership development and higher productivity.

THE COMPROMISE

A linear equation that is represented in the variables X and Y which are "unknown" until solved is not as complicated as in the case of Gen X and Gen Y. Gen X are linear, punctual, and structured while millennials can be nonlinear and unstructured. What motivates the two generations are completely different things, but there is nothing that communication cannot fix, even if Gen X feel that they are speaking a language that millennials are not wired to comprehend.

What we notice in today's world is that many senior executives who run companies are delaying necessary changes in their HR and performance review practices for the sake of short-term requirements. Instead, the focus should reside on long-term growth that should be achieved through crucial culture changes.

If companies want to do a better job of retaining millennials, it is important for them to understand what motivates Gen Y and what does not so that they can achieve a balance between the two. Millennials, to a great extent, desire the same things from their employers as most generations. They ultimately seek growth opportunities, great employers and jobs that are well-suited for their talents and interests. Companies that can adopt a performance measurement system that takes into account a lot of these factors will likely gain the loyalty of millennial workers.

The use of technology to improve performance review procedures is critical to making the most out of the process. Regular feedback that Gen Y values so much doesn't always need to be delivered face-to-face. Instead, companies should start looking into digital and other ways to generate a dynamic feedback system that leads to performance improvement. Without the burden of paperwork, managers can then focus on helping their direct reportees improve for the future.

In the talent management and development process, promising millennials should be trained, promoted and empowered so they are motivated and engaged. However, most HR systems today tend to offer overviews of the employees, their background and their performance, but often they don't capture talented employees' motivations. According to a survey by WorldatWork, Loyola University, and Hay Group, the key elements that impact employee engagement and motivation include career planning, work/life balance and quality of work.

Managers need to be equipped with effective tools to easily make smart, effective and efficient decisions, including performance and goal data. Managers should have an overview of the average compensation of top performers among their peers and in the marketplace. Besides consistent and ongoing feedback, it is crucial to have software that tracks employees' individual goals and performance and captures their career development.

Millennials have a strong appetite for learning as they spend most of their time developing new skills and absorbing all sorts of new information and experiences at the job. Education has been offered as a reward for employees over the years with emphasis by the HR team that the field of study should be relevant to employees' core business and job description. However, have employers considered how motivating it could be if the reward was to study a subject of general interest (such as creative writing, learning a new language, or a new skill) that benefits the employees' personal development in a broader sense? In addition to that, training and development programmes—ones that primarily use coaching and mentorship—attract Gen Y. A study has shown that employees most committed to their organisation put in 57% more effort and are 87% less likely to consider resigning.

According to a TriNet study on the performance review process for millennials, the key takeaways emphasized specific feedback that is ongoing and consistent—feedback that encourages a two-way-street conversation that is both objective in its criticism and forward-looking.

There is an evident need for reviewing HR Systems. HR systems that are generally used by businesses today are sometimes sophisticated yet inefficient. Adopting visually attractive and easy-to-use people management software could possibly encourage and engage employees to quickly fill out and review performance reviews while still delivering the data which the HR department needs to develop high-impact reports and analytics. Gen Y expects people management solutions to reflect the current smart systems that they use in their personal lives.

Company performance and employee management strategies are meant to engage and motivate employees, retain top performers and improve the company's efficiency overall. Several organisations have already embraced a new dawn and started seeking alternatives to their old manual processes of performance management which often involved documents and spreadsheets. Others are in the process of implementing technologies such as HRMS (Human Resource Management Systems). These existing systems and softwares can also overwhelm employees with features and underwhelm them with poor design. Leaders need critical business intelligence to make quick decisions that impact their organisational performance.

When companies can adjust their recognition programmes appropriately, this can impact business performance greatly/ exponentially/

considerably. According to Glassdoor.com, more than 80% of employees said they were motivated to work harder and stay at their jobs longer when they received appreciation for their work.

TIPS WORTHY OF CONSIDERATION:

#1 Some of the steps companies can take to enhance their performance management approach is to create development plans with clear planning, giving feedback on individual projects, offering different incentives that appeal to millennials, and providing mentoring programmes for employees to meet and work with senior management.

#2 Another crucial point of consideration is the adoption of online technologies to encourage an open culture and the provision of coaching to managers on how to manage Gen Y. Most importantly, companies should devise ways of providing employees with constant feedback about work—informally and formally—and not wait until the annual appraisal as has typically been the case when managing previous generations

#3 In order to generate successful engagement monitoring and progress, managers should also be given appropriate discretion and authority in managing employees. Since Gen Y tend to be highly relationship based, they require frequent and specific feedback. Which means managers should be entrusted with the power to be flexible in their approach but remain professional.

> *"Communication is key, our generation nourishes over honest feedback, one that clearly highlights positive improvements on key competencies."*

Chapter Four

IT'S NOT ABOUT PROMOTIONS, IT'S ABOUT PURPOSE

Mrs. Hope

"*B*eauty is in the eyes of the beholder.' Each person perceives the source of happiness and rejoices it differently. This is also true for each collective group of people like a generation that does 'things' in a different way. The thrill that we get as Generation Xers when we get promoted, the sweets that we distribute, and the feasts that our Arabian warm culture produces to celebrate the promotion of someone is not at all the thrill and excitement of a millennial when they get promoted. To this generation, purpose comes first. Everyday becomes a celebration if faced with a new challenge that makes them *grow* and *contribute* to the overall direction of an organisation. What defines a promotion thus becomes of utmost importance. Let me converse with Saj and find out more about what they mean by it. What do they value?

I thoroughly enjoyed my conversation with her the other day about performance appraisals and truly felt that our performance management system needs to be revamped. I am now ever so determined to play a vital role in pushing the big boss to pay more attention to this and bring an HR consultant to come and help us with this. We need *change*, and we need it *soon*. I am now petrified at the thought of promotions. After this whole performance appraisal shebang that has just happened, I wonder how staff will react to the few promotions that will be announced. Especially since most of them worked very hard and feel entitled to them. Deep down inside a voice tells me it's not going to be so bad, but it will be worse not to fix things from the root. It is not the promotions and the numbers that scare me. They don't care much about that. I need to focus on what they care about. Creating purpose and drive. Changing the chore of what they do and how they do it. Training the line managers to coach these youngsters to forge their way through their career ladders. Creating that sense of growth by genuine links between daily work and their overall purpose in the company. Giving them a *voice* at the decision-making table. But how do I do this for this large pool of youngsters in a seamless way? Man, I really need help!

> "What we are good at, and the practice of this, has an important impact on how we feel about our day to day experience of work. The level of satisfaction that we have from the activities we perform everyday influences our overall sense of well-being."

And what better help can I get than listening to my favourite millennial? This time, I will not leave it to chance. I shall call her in and ask her to assist me. I shall ask her to help me find ways in which her colleagues and her can feel part of the story—part of the creation of their own self-growth and the organisation's path to its own future. I will ask them to draw the path for me as to how they visualize it, and maybe we can strike a deal with management. I am so worried that the boss doesn't take it seriously, but I pray that by now he realizes that this is our only way forward and that their voice is better than anyone else's. Let them lead since leadership to them is not defined by managing staff but rather managing from any position they are in, thus achieving the overall objective. That is their definition of leadership, and that is what I shall present to Saj now... That is, therefore, the true 'promotion' they seek.

I pick up the phone to call her in. No response. Then I remember that she must be sitting on that bean bag I managed to get for the new quiet room on the tenth floor. So I sent her a text message. And there she was, responding instantly with a thumbs-up, meaning she would see me in a second."

Saj

"Not sure if I want to drive to work this morning. I remember experiencing these exact same emotions last year when promotions were announced and my name had no place amidst the list. I recall writing a letter to my superior, wondering if we could sit and discuss 'what went wrong' and 'what could I have done differently'. I was so confused. I felt blindsided because my appraisal had gone so well. I kept playing the tape in my mind over and over again as to how I would approach the whole situation and what kind of questions I would ask, making sure my argument would not come across as a battle of 'entitlement'. That word was and still is a *taboo* for my generation. Needless to say, that discussion that I had rehearsed for many nights never happened. I remember regretting writing a letter because the only feedback I got out of it is that my generation is impatient and full of demands.

I'm at a crossroad once again, but this time I am even more confused. I am starting to question *what* the leadership of this organisation is looking for. What type of social skills do they expect? Are they looking for employees that are cooperative and easy-going? Ones that conform to the rules and tread carefully when sharing their opinions? Because in all honesty, I am more of a 'be innovative and push for excellence' kind of employee. I admit that I am never hesitant in challenging the system if I perceive that work can be performed with greater efficiency. Although our organisation and its leaders trumpet the importance of quality and creativity, I am not sure our organisational culture is ready for it. I am starting to think that the management may prefer people who get along with others instead of being the forerunner and champion of new and innovative ideas. I understand the value of collaborative behaviour and its importance in maximizing business performance, but I am also a firm believer of what makes a 'true asset', and 'that' certainly cannot be measured based on interpersonal skills alone.

Perhaps the 'quality of work' and 'driving results' are not equally as important as the 'time served' and 'quantity delivered'. I might have misunderstood the parameters of promotion eligibility and criteria. In fact, being overly dedicated might be doing me a disservice. If I am willing to do twice the work for half the pay, it would be ridiculous to promote me, especially if I am still at the phase of having to prove myself around here.

What harms my generation the most is not the mere perception that we can do the job better or faster, but it is often our selfish plot of wanting to be the 'overachiever' and doing ten times the work, thinking that it will guarantee us a promotion. I confess that sometimes we do lose track of the bigger picture- which is the holistic improvement of organisational performance and achieving bottom-line profits. Another thing that we clearly lack due to our youthful exuberance is the ability and experience to play 'office politics'. There is a great chance that management has already decided the names up in line for a promotion far ahead of our performance review meetings. Sigh... I'm trying to nudge that negative yet very possible thought away.

Getting in my car as it is almost 7:15 am, I decide not to sit around thinking about this anymore. I will get over it the same way I got over it last year. As I make my way to the office, I decide that I want to avoid the gathering currently going on in the pantry. I am sure many millennials are displeased with the news. Instead of ruffling feathers, joining the negativity and most likely contributing to it, I would rather sit in a quiet place with my laptop and headphones, muting everything around but the sound of Coldplay in my ears.

Shuffling through my music, I get a text message notification. My heart drops. So she wants to see me. I always took on the habit of venting first. This time I am anxious to hear her out. I wonder if I have the courage to express my thoughts this time. My mind decides, however, I shall not speak from a stance of defeat."

A shared sense of purpose, recognition and rewards are the cornerstones of an effective and dynamic millennial talent management strategy.

Demonstrating appreciation to your employees for their contribution to your business can boost levels of staff satisfaction and loyalty. However, most companies do not understand or appreciate the importance of establishing reward systems that are in line with the values of millennials. This slow adaptation stifles business growth due to a failure to establish a market-responsive company culture where staff recognize and encourage one another. It will always remain true that monetary incentives are a necessity, but with millennials demanding a different kind of performance reward and recognition system that is more suited to their agenda of purpose over promotions, many companies have their work cut out for them.

It is important that business leaders go beyond just incentivising their top performers with pecuniary rewards. Some studies have in fact revealed that a large majority of employees feel undervalued, mainly due to a lack of recognition. It has been proven in numerous studies, including a survey recently conducted by Glassdoor, in which it was found that employees said they were motivated to work harder and stay at their jobs longer when they received appreciation for their work.

It is fascinating to think that the employee recognition market is estimated to be at around 46 billion US Dollars. This is attributed to companies buying employees gold watches, plaques and pins, or spending revenues on thank-you awards and other incentive schemes. Approximately 1-2% of their payroll is reportedly spent on such incentives and recognition programmes which clearly shows how huge this market is. Another surprising fact is that roughly 87% of the recognition programmes are centered on tenure. This further proves that people are predominant-

> *"The capacity to attract, retain and manage executive talent does not depend on the compensation package, but rather on our ability to create a sense of belonging to an organization that offers a long-term relationship and a professional development opportunity, and that has a clear conception of itself, of what it wants to be, and of how to achieve it."* — ARMANDO GARZA SADA

ly rewarded for simply "sticking around" and not necessarily because of the impact or contribution they have made towards the success of the businesses. Whether or not time spent working for the company has proven fruitful, the accolade is a different matter completely. It seems as though companies are still stuck with legacy systems that have no relevance in today's work environment. And especially not for our millennial workforce!

Gone are the days when labour unions used to force companies to give employees service awards for tenure, but a large number of companies still have the same reward systems in place. Ultimately, researchers concluded that tenure-based rewards systems have virtually no impact on organisational performance, and they also found that about two-thirds of employees in the companies surveyed were actually aware that those were old-school incentives. Millennials don't seem too concerned about such programmes because they simply don't subscribe to the idea of working for an employer for a long time if not offered real self-development and growth opportunities.

As you are now aware, millennials have values that are very different from previous generations, meaning that a different approach needs to be taken into account in order to ensure that organisations are keeping this all-important, youthful workforce happy and productive.

Millennials want feedback and acknowledgment regularly, and preferably in real-time. Although this is not always feasible, it's important for managers to try to schedule feedback sessions as close as possible to the actions they are rewarding in order to reinforce the behaviours they want to encourage.

Now you might be wondering how you can effectively modify or change your recognition programme to accommodate your Gen Y employees. Well, you are not alone in such contemplations. A good example of a company that is taking steps to re-calibrate its incentive and rewards schemes is Deloitte. At this very successful company, it is reported that almost half of the client-facing workforce is comprised of millennials. In an attempt to ensure that this important group is motivated, Deloitte has created a comprehensive onboarding programme specifically for Gen Y recruits. The incentive programme they put in place reinforces the company's core beliefs, simulates the feel of working on a client team, teaches network-building skills, and eventually, focuses on professional development in the specific business unit the millennial joined. Almost all the participants they surveyed after implementing these programmes confirmed that the interactive simulations, role-plays, small-group teams, and even video games that are incorporated are largely the reason why they feel appreciated and consequently loyal to the company.

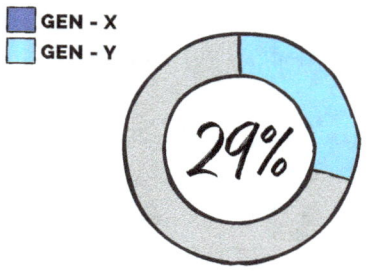

PERCENTAGE OF MILLENNIALS THAT ARE ENGAGED WITH THEIR JOB
SOURCE: 2016 Gallup Report

Human resources personnel spend enormous amounts of time researching and implementing employee benefits that they believe will strengthen a company's culture. However, it's often the case that a lack of engagement with benefits is generally due to a lack of knowledge. HR technology can make benefits more approachable, upfront, encouraging and manageable in the long-term. Since many employees actually don't take advantage of the opportunities, some companies offer in terms of vacation days, health breaks, etc. Up-to-date systems allow companies to have better training opportunities and to make it easy for employees to monitor their own benefit usage. It's not just about payroll and performance management systems but HR systems that make it easier to manage people. The right kind of HR technology platforms can help rather than hinder communication and connectivity which plays a big role in introducing company culture changes.

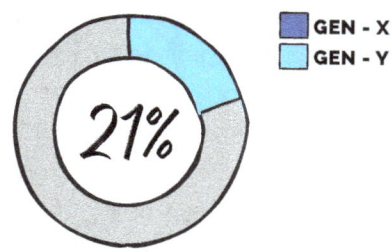

PERCENTAGE OF MILLENNIALS THAT CHANGED JOBS WITHIN 2016

That's more than three times the number of non-millennials. This millennial turnover is costing the U.S. economy $30.5 billion annually

SOURCE: 2016 Gallup Report

Businesses can often underestimate the impact that work can have on an individual's personal life. That is why it is crucial for employers to show that they recognize and understand the need for a healthy work-life balance. In our fast-paced lives, it can be difficult to find time for activities like employee recognition. And with only so much bandwidth available to focus on their teams, managers often turn their attention to employees who need extra support to succeed, assuming their top-performers are just fine on their own. What they often overlook is the fact that even top-performing employees also need to be acknowledged frequently so that they can stay motivated.

Gen Y Thoughts

The main reason why we millennials find the process of an annual performance review to be flawed is due to it causing some sort of a "feedback vacuum" where we are left in the dark for months with little or no feedback on our performance and quality of work for the sake of our managers "saving the talk and appraisal" for the time when it is due. It baffles me how huge organisations around the region still inject massive budgets into HR and management systems that are successfully alienating young talent, to say the least.

"A vision that is shaped by aligning our passion, our abilities and our context seems a good place to start, in order to give ourselves the flexibility of going through new paths creatively."

When will the world understand that one size never fits all and that there is an evident need for employees and managers to interact and communicate in a much more fluid and flexible manner.

There is an evident culture of managers not coming to grips with giving feedback. This resistance to change is puzzling when you come to think about it. Don't organisations ultimately wish to retain their staff and capitalise on the talents within to best achieve organisational objectives? Isn't it the ultimate win-win situation when you embrace change that motivates and satisfies the main pillars that no organisation can function without?

Something as simple as the "feedback process"—how often and how relevant—makes a huge difference and translates into far more engagement and motivation.

When the traditional performance review process came into the picture 60 years ago, it made sense because most of the workforce was

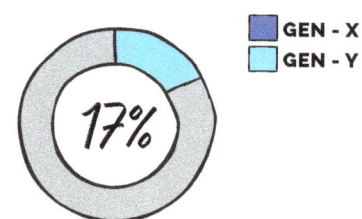

GEN - X
GEN - Y

17%

PERCENTAGE OF MILLENNIALS THAT SAY THEY WOULD LIKE TO SHARE THEIR EXPERIENCE WITH THEIR TEAM.

heavily engaged in manufacturing. So not only have we witnessed a changing workforce dynamic, but we are facing an accelerated change of pace that was almost non-existent before.

The bottom line is that our generation wants constant feedback. We do not view this process as a competitive evaluation that makes us feel like we are part of The Hunger Games. We want constant coaching, mentoring and development. The future calls for nothing less than full participation to meet such necessary demands that will eventually result in a culture where trust can flourish.

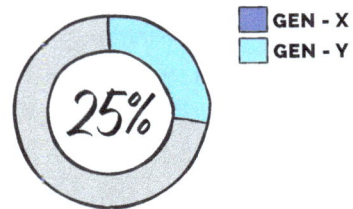

PERCENTAGE OF MILLENNIALS THAT SAY THEY WOULD LIKE TO SHARE THEIR REWARDS WITH THEIR FAMILY AND FRIENDS.
SOURCE: 2016 Gallup Report

Gen X Speaking

This time of the year is always a very negative one where the importance of the "big picture" loses its way and is devoured by the "self". Self-interest and personal gain become a priority, and all the slogans of teamwork and complementing each other diminish. Is this something I can accept or should learn to accept as part of human nature? And can I justify it? I think I must learn to accept the human factors and natural instincts of self-defense and people not seeing their own blind spots. Millennials are no different, but in addition to the human instinctive reactions, they have different needs. Their expectations, in fact, can be managed by earlier communication and engagement in an overall purpose. Leading their own growth—in line with organisational objectives and growth—is one path. Moreover, determining their own rewards, if not financial, can be a huge advantage that lies in front of Gen X managers to offer.

THE COMPROMISE

W henever millennials are asked about their potential for a promotion, they should not be instantly discouraged and made to feel that they have an unjustified sense of entitlement. This is because millennials having such expectations can actually be leveraged into a situation where businesses capitalise on this energy, enthusiasm, and passion—making it a win-win-situation for everyone. For instance, if the roadmap for a promotion was clearly drawn, and a set of KPIs to be accomplished properly outlined, this would only get employees more engaged and focused. Millennials simply want to know what is expected of them.

Approximately a third of millennials are actually engaged in their job with the remainder being disengaged. Twhis disengagement indicates that they are emotionally not present, and in a world where employees are battling to retain the best talent, it's detrimental for companies to let young workers exit their companies with a chip on their shoulders. Remember that in the internet age, employees can revert to social media outlets to vent their frustrations and in the process damage the reputation of the company. Therefore, employers need to seriously consider investing a little more time into implementing effective engagement plans.

Purpose, Passion and Pay are three words that should help managers set objectives. Workplaces that serve the human factor and strive to make a positive societal impact are the most sought after by millennials.

"Allow your passion to become your purpose, and it will one day, become your profession."

The majority of millennials are more inclined to work for organisations that act responsibly and ethically. Finding meaning in what they do largely impacts workers' productivity. Purpose is essentially output related. Millennials factor creativity in this equation in the satisfaction equation. Flexibility, variety and freedom are some of the most important elements that HR professionals and management teams should consider. Some millennials may be lured by attractive pay packages when they initially accept a job offer, but it's usually only a matter of time before they realize that a huge salary won't suffice on its own.

Ben Horowitz once stated that it is much easier for us to realize what we're good at instead of what we are passionate about since passion may change over time. If we look into passion, then we are looking more precisely into "The Happiness Hypothesis" as described by Haidt's—a "state of total immersion in a task that is challenging yet closely matched to one's abilities. It is what people sometimes call 'being in the zone'".

Millennials define success as their ability to transform passion into achievements or even bigger so, into a career—and that is the ultimate incentive.

TIPS WORTHY OF CONSIDERATION:

#1 Change your management style. Employers need to realize that millennials would gladly trade a well-paid and secure job for a riskier one that is more aligned with their passions. Passion for bringing about positive change is what qualifies people as "change-makers".

#2 Change your rewards. It is important to highlight the key metrics that help managers understand how to better retain millennial talent. It is through understanding the inverse relationship between what employees want, their levels of job satisfaction, and what they currently have and their present satisfaction levels.

#3 Recognise differences. Millennials' preferred approach towards rewards and recognition in the workplace is training and development opportunities plus a focus on developing their individual skills, rather than on monetary rewards and recognition programmes. The latter do not offer much in the way of career and personal development.

Chapter Five
EXITING THE WORKPLACE

Mrs. Hope

"*I* am very worried about the news that our HR just gave me. Two of the best candidates we got in last insourcing are leaving. Together! And through the grapevine I heard three more are thinking about it. Leave alone all the other kids that have been coming to me for advice and guidance. Why do they leave? HR conducted exit interviews with them to answer that very question. But it's very hard to get people to be totally candid and forthcoming during exit interviews because most of them don't want to burn their bridges. They want to leave on good terms, so they often won't say anything negative or revealing. What do we do to get around this? We could use an outside third party to conduct exit interviews... but will that solve the problem? I don't think so. We need to do more. Our middle managers who are losing their employees need to know why. Millennials are not coming to work only to earn. Yet the sole part of the manager's job is to help them earn. We have to turn the reasons millennials leave into reasons they will stay and work harder. We cannot wait until millennials start thinking about leaving to ask these questions and ask them what the problem *was*. Communicating clearly and asking them what will make them stay should be a conversation that starts from day one and continues every single day. Should we cater to their every whim? Of course not. But millennials need to know that somebody knows what they want and need, somebody cares, and somebody is going to work with them to help them earn more and grow.

The reality is that we can't do everything for everybody. If we are talking with them about how to meet their needs and wants on an ongoing basis, they are much more likely to talk with us about those key points when they are trying to decide whether to leave or stay. There is a level of job satisfaction for each person and each job performed. What does happiness mean to these millennials? I have enough worries with my teenage daughter who will be a Gen-Z catastrophe, but I cannot run away from this. The positive nature in me seeks to face this challenge and go to the source of their unhappiness and work on it. Not everyone can be satisfied with their job. A survey conducted by Right Management in the US revealed that 65% of individuals that were surveyed were either somewhat or totally unsatisfied with their jobs. This is a worldwide problem though. A Mercer study of 30,000 workers worldwide shows that between 28% and 56% of workers around the globe want to leave their jobs. That's a startling figure! With all this unhappiness, I cannot cease to wonder what the causes and reactions are. What is the impact of all this unhappiness on not only the office ambiance and dynamics but sheer productivity on a daily basis? Are employees acting? Pretending? Or what?! Children can express their anger physically and through direct verbal demands, stomp their feet on the floor and scream, but what can employees do? We must find ways to identify that discontent and hopefully address it before it goes too far.

This time, there will be no conversation with my favorite millennial... There will be me going to the executive management meeting this week and showing them the proposal I have been working on—not alone but with my millennial ambassadors. I will finally get to show all our findings, all our plans which will elevate this organisation and make it indeed the 'employer of choice' and give it the 'thumbs-up' and 'likes' by any millennial. A plan that will make all three generations work in sync and produce the best for our company, for our country and for the world at large. I pray that I have managed to lay the foundation of thought and desire to change what we do because *change* and *evolution* are the only choices we have. Embracing them and being proactive is a sign of being positive about venturing into a current reality and an exciting future that lies ahead for our labour market. However, I will do this the millennial way. They shall present because we are showing case studies, videos, storyboards and projects that they worked on and have proven their arguments by themselves. There are only 30 minutes left. I better make sure Saj and her workmates are ready. Let me message her so they can go to the boardroom and prepare."

Saj

"Since I was little, my parents reinforced the idea that I could be anything I had wished to become and that 'the sky is the limit.' I cannot reinforce how such encouraging words and actions had a lot to do with my perspective on what comprises a fulfilling career. Growing up, we were constantly in pursuit of something special—we were brought up with the idea that 'life is too short' and that we should not stop looking until we find '*it*'. So what exactly is '*it*'?

'*It*' is a life that had all our desires seamlessly coexisting—*it* being fulfillment; '*it*' being meaning-ful; '*it*' being magical; '*it*' is what we were meant to be doing; and '*it*' is doing what we love to do without it feeling tedious.

'*It*' was even more glorified when others around us got the grasp of it: the school-drop-outs-turned-millionaires, the visionaries, and the wonderers. Such living examples created that eagerness that *we too* could make a living out of something we care about or something we are exceptionally good at. So why settle for this boring by-the-book adulthood when we can chase our dreams?

All our lives, we heard our parents and grandparents fuss about a life sentenced to hard work and savings for the time they would retire. Witnessing that, I swore to never do the same.

Some of us were lucky enough to spend a few months or years abroad, which alone shaped our vision and perspective of what is acceptable and what is not. Today's world of work is definitely the latter. Most of us do not want to be anchored to a desk for a specific number of minimum hours. Most of us do not speak the language of political nuances planted within the roots of our companies. Most of us would not pledge our loyalty if we are not active players in making a difference or if we are constantly reminded that we are 'not the boss' and that we cannot influence anything–except to do the required work. Most of us do not have the patience or desire to wait for a gold watch' at the end of our years of service.

Most of us want *change*–and if it is not part of the menu, we will add it!

It is about time to put to sleep all rumours of millennials being lazy and entitled and refer to us as 'empowered' instead. We will not accept taking our growth and development for granted. We do not waste time. If the company is not willing to facilitate this for us, we will take our careers into our own hands.

So, *no*, we are not temperamental because we feel like it. We seek to be challenged in ways that we are used to, in ways that are daring! There is no shame in wanting something more. We won't settle because everyone around us is used to it. 'Everyone around us' might have lived with different goals, looking to fill different needs, and aspiring different desires.

Suddenly, I snap out of my thoughts and hope to have the courage to state all that we wish to convey to the management. I pray that we are understood and not have to leave the boardroom feeling denigrated. A glimpse of hope radiates on my smartphone screen, a reminder that Mrs. Hope will be on our side. I had better pick up the pace and hurry downstairs. *'It will be good'*–an inner voice reassures me. Otherwise I will have no option but to make my exit too, which is the last thing I want to do."

P ersonal values have the greatest influence on millennials' decision-making on a job. The pursuit of opportunities for leadership development and career advancement does not stop with this breed. When Gen Y workers feel that they do not possess a clear path for career advancement and development, they are prone to make an exit in quest of greener pastures.

Millennials often switch jobs or even careers due to financial incentives. But more so, for a need of an innovative work environment. We now know that Gen Y workers have a strong inclination towards a flexible work life. A huge chunk of the millennial workforce is already largely employed remotely or as freelancers who prefer to work from home or the coffee shop on days they don't have meetings to attend. If they have just started their families, they also feel the need to have sufficient time with their families and have a harmonious work-life balance.

Depending on their interests, personal traits and behavioural dispositions, millennials want to work on schedules that are best suited to their lifestyle choices and preferences. This should not be mistaken for a sense of entitlement or seen as having unreasonable demands but rather a need for flexibility within the workplace that allows them to preserve their sense of identity and individuality. As long as they achieve the results and meet the organisational expectations as far as work execution is concerned, the emphasis should not be placed on when or where they work. With this in mind, it is difficult not to agree with the growing consensus that most Gen Y workers exit the workplace due to a lack of flexibility on their employer's part. Some HR professionals have recommended that companies take a different approach to their talent-retaining strategies by, for instance, shifting the focus from stringent start and end times but still keeping the project deadlines fixed. This will allow millennials to have the flexibility to achieve work-integration that makes sense for their specific situations, which is ultimately crucial to sustaining their motivation, productivity, morale, loyalty, sense of worthiness and recognition.

Above all, research seems to suggest that millennials are constantly seeking and searching for companies whose values align with their own personal principles. Working for companies that have a culture which promote positivity and well-being in and out of the office is what

Gen Y workers want. Employers that support workers in their personal and professional lives seem to be the most sought after. It quickly becomes evident why some employers consider millennials a flight risk because they are unwilling to settle for less than a company with great values, one that takes its corporate responsibilities seriously, and promotes inclusivity and growth.

Research finds two-thirds of millennials plan to leave their current organisation by 2020. One-quarter see themselves elsewhere within the next year. These are dangerous and staggering statistics since this generation is the *stayers*—baby boomers being the *leavers* with Gen X *in between*. While one could argue that young workers have always been inclined to job hop—and it has become widely acceptable to do so—their reasons for restlessness may have changed. Millennials are unhappy about the insufficient opportunities given to them to develop their leadership skills. According to the fifth annual Global Millennials survey cited on Bloomberg, for which Deloitte reached out to nearly 7,700 working, college-educated professionals in 29 countries, 63% of respondents said their leadership skills are not being fully developed. This apparently is one the primary reasons behind their willingness to leave. While 71% of those likely to leave in the next two years are dissatisfied with how their leadership skills are being developed, that number drops to 54% amongst those who are planning to stay beyond 2020.

"They want a job that fuels their sense of purpose and a manager who shows them how their efforts advance the company's mission. By meeting Millennials' need for purpose, leaders and managers are more likely to retain these workers."

Punit Renjen, Chief Executive Officer of Deloitte Global, told Bloomberg that young workers' pursuit of leadership skills even at the expense of switching jobs is a new phenomenon. With automation and the advent of technology, organisations are being flattened, and thus there are no *real* opportunities for leadership practice. Organisations have removed levels of bureaucracy, which means there's not much of a corporate ladder to climb anymore. This is a *huge* dilemma that we face today. The biggest driver of disengagement is people feeling like they're stuck in a job and there's nothing for them there, so it becomes much easier to find progression by shifting to a new organisation and creating that jump. Rather than waiting for things to slowly happen where they are stuck. A recent Gallup poll shows that 60% of millennials would consider leaving their jobs if they didn't feel engaged at work—and only half plan to be with the same company a year from now.

It is not that these millennials enjoy leaving. They want to stay at work. But they cannot stay when they feel their values and work-life balance are compromised. A report on millennials says that this gener-

IN AN UNCERTAIN ENVIRONMENT, TURNOVER WILL LIKEY REMAIN HIGH

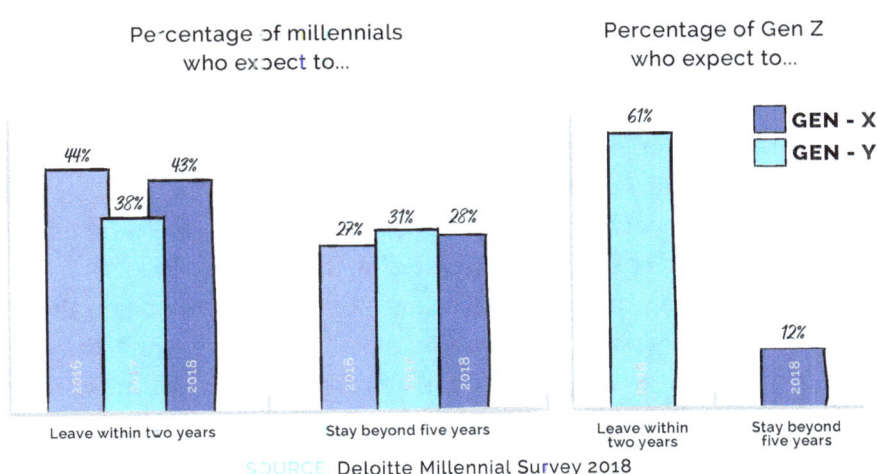

SOURCE: Deloitte Millennial Survey 2018

ation needs to find meaning in their work. Seventy-one percent of millennials who know what their organisation stands for and what makes it different from its competitors say they plan to stay with their company for at least another year. Eighty-seven percent of millennials surveyed rate professional or career growth and development opportunities as important to them in a job, and 68% of millennials who strongly agree they have had opportunities at work to learn and grow in the past year plan to be with their organisation for at least another year. A full 93% of millennials said they had to leave their job to get a new role. One contributing factor was thought to be that millennials do not feel comfortable approaching their managers when they desire progress or something new.

According to a 2014 Allstate-National Journal Heartland Monitor

Poll, roughly 71% of baby boomers reported that achieving success in a career is necessary to living a good life, as compared to 91% of millennials. A PWC study also backs these claims by suggesting that millennials do not believe that productivity should be measured by the number of hours worked at the office, but by the output of the work performed. They view work as a "thing" and not a "place".

We need to be preemptive in our approach to effectively address this problem. Waiting until millennials have already secured other opportunities and decided firmly to resign is like trying to address the symptoms instead of understanding the root cause of the disease. A retrospective approach only leaves companies short of worthy talent and brand ambassadors. It is to be expected that when those employees leave, they will undoubtedly make disclosures to people about their reasons for leaving, which could seriously deter future prospects from wanting to work for those companies.

HR personnel and management should have an up-to-date retention strategy guide from the onset of recruitment. Millennials need to be certain that employers are aware of their aspirations and that the companies care enough to consider these aspects in the way they cultivate employer-employee relations. Of course, realistically, no company can ever satisfy each individual employee's needs, but they can certainly make an effort to evaluate those same needs and align them with the company's overall goals to enable the employee to produce the best value for the company while maintaining a shared vision..

Gen Y Speaking

Numerous reasons cause millennials *to find the exit doors very attractive*. At the forefront of these reasons is the realisation that they are not in the right role. After a period of time, they comprehend that the organisation's mission and values do not resonate with their own. Many millennials choose to make that call after realizing that they are not as appreciated as they would have hoped to be. When their feedback is not heard—or their ideas are not necessarily entertained or welcomed—they eventually feel like whatever they bring to the table does not matter. Others hope for clear guidance and a proper succession plan to be communicated, only to realise there isn't one and that they will most probably be pigeonholed in the same role for a long time.

The biggest enemy to millennials is boredom and feeling redundant at the job. They do not speak the language of routine very well. Feeling stagnant and intellectually defeated rather than stimulated is a big factor contributing to rapidly building frustration and an unwavering decision towards leaving their jobs behind.

Millennials are not narcissistic, but rather overlooked. What they mostly seek in a work culture is to work in a community with like-minded people and employees who understand the demands of living in a digitalised world. If a millennial is expected to be prepared to pick up the phone from their nightstand to respond to a midnight work email, they would at least expect that the other side would be someone who would listen to their thoughts in the morning.

"You can quit your job, but can't quit your calling"

Gen X Speaking

You are either *in* or *out*. One word that separates the "job hoppers" bunch from the more stable ones is engagement. Being engaged and feeling valued is the number one reason for employee loyalty. Millennials cannot stay if they feel that their values and their work-life balance are being compromised. Neither can they be retained if they feel unable to communicate freely and are held back by information silos. 93% of millennials pointed out that they would consider leaving their jobs if they were uncomfortable approaching their managers regarding career progress or requiring more/less work.

If millennials lack the sense of being challenged at the job, they become complacent. Studies have shown that the average time spent at a job is 1.3 years. The dilemma lies here. In the past, previous generations used to feel incentivised knowing that their company was taking good care of them, i.e. if they did the job well, this would lead to a promotion and ultimately a good pension. The reality is no longer that. Given the current market conditions, millennials are not bound to any traditional incentive to be retained with the exception of doing meaningful work and having to develop their skills and competencies. If the company fails to provide the latter, they have every reason to hop to the next opportunity to grow themselves elsewhere.

THE COMPROMISE:
CREATING A COHESIVE COMPANY CULTURE
THAT PROMOTES STAFF RETENTION

E quipped with the necessary knowledge and facts, employees should swiftly move towards organisational change to strengthen their base as solid corporations. Bentley University's Center for Women & Business (CWB) conducted a survey of 1,000 college-educated men and women born since 1980 to provide a more in-depth picture of the career aspirations of millennials and the values driving those aspirations. They found that it is important to let millennials

IT'S NOT ABOUT THE PAYCHECK

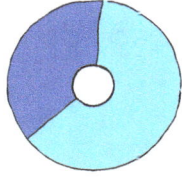 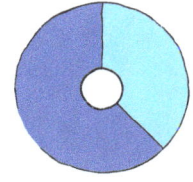 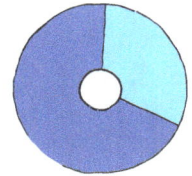

58%	45%	35%
would accept a 15% pay cut if it meant working for a company "with values like [their] own"	would take the same pay cut for a job that has an environmental or social impact	would do so for an organization that has a commitment to corporate social responsibility

 GEN - X GEN - Y   SOURCE: Net Impact Survey, 2012

know that their work matters. They also highlighted the importance of providing Gen Y employees with flexible work arrangements, including parental leave that takes into consideration personal circumstances. Furthermore, the study revealed that companies ought to create multiple paths and timeframes for individuals to reach leadership positions.

Millennials expect a more people-oriented, gender-neutral culture.

They want career paths that allow them to be true to their personal and family values. In addition, being underpaid is a hot topic of debate as it is often deemed as being subject to perspective and personal interpretation. A lack of opportunity to ascend the corporate ladder is another major cause of dissatisfaction which ultimately leads to employees leaving those companies which don't address such concerns.

In addition, millennials cite poor management as one of the prominent reasons for leaving particular companies. Bosses who aren't at least managing their employees well demotivate them, cost the company money, and end up causing the best employees to leave. Companies should consider what elements of their employees' work are monotonous and uninteresting and try to make employees more engaged by perhaps adopting better technological deployment of some tasks to make them more engaging. Feeling stagnant and intellectually defeated rather than stimulated is a big factor contributing to the desertion of jobs by millennials. Millennials make the point that inspiring leadership or lack thereof really influences the decisions that employees make when considering long-term career prospects under the servitude of a particular company.

TIPS WORTHY OF CONSIDERATION:

#1 Show more flexibility: Let go of Gen X and previous generation's infatuation with rigid work hours and physical workplace systems. It's tough, but learn to let go and embrace new working styles while measuring results at all times.

#2 Communicate and engage them: Involve millennials in the decision-making either through new social media techniques, digital organisational platforms, or forums and debates. Engage them and let their voices be heard.

#3 Pay close attention to personal interests: Companies that don't pay close attention or take personal interest in the aspirations and ideals of millennials in the workplace are bound to miss out on excellent opportunities to retain employees and consequently retard their business growth and competitiveness in a market which will soon be predominantly made up of millennial workers.

#4 Develop them: Spend time in coaching and mentoring them to build their decision-making and interpersonal skills in addition to investing in their education and growth.

"The secret of change is to focus all of your energy, not on fighting the old, but on building the new"

— SORCRATES

CONCLUSION

What is clear by now is that we face an "upside reality" of our labour markets in which jobs are fewer, salaries are competitive, job stability is non-existent, and career growth is suffering Yet there s an ongoing surging demand and pressure for flexibility in the workplace as we live in a world where technology has allowed the world to amalgamate. International opportunities are plenty and markets are open. The journey of a millennial in the labour markets of today is changing the shape of HR systems and corporate cultures. Millennials have exceeded their predecessors now in terms of numbers. This is a reality and will become more so since Generation-Z has offcially entered the workforce. It is thus vital to keep the direction going forward and not to abide by the systems that we have once invested so much in because it simply what suited the generations that *passed.*

We have learned that it is a process. We have to change our culture, hiring practices and engagement incrementally in order to create a strong team of varied generations. We must hold employees accountable but at the same time give them opportunities, mentoring, coaching and practical experiences. We must communicate more effectively—provide real-time feedback, frequent check-ins, detailed reviews, and most of all, invest in our teams and build mutual commitment to team, company and industry at large.

Millennials are at the outset of their careers, but as boomers are making their way to retirement, there is a clear upward mobility that is allowing millennials to take over management role. Hence, investment and development in future business leaders is essential for business growth and stability. Career progression is *key* to this generation, and drawing a clear path to progression is the ultimate motivator.

What is certain is that employers, economists, leaders and scholars need to realize the impact of the mass wave of Gen Yers that is poised to influence the world of work in an unprecedented fashion.

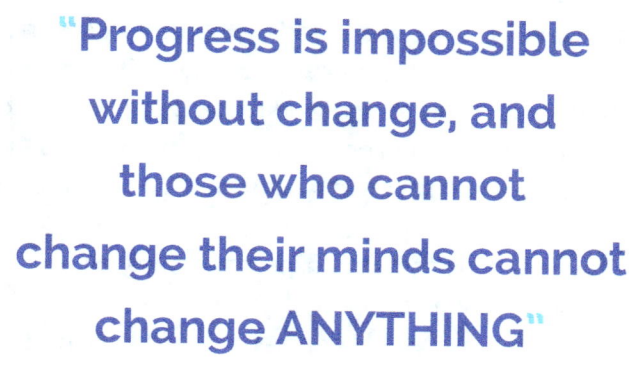

"Progress is impossible without change, and those who cannot change their minds cannot change ANYTHING"

— GEORGE BERNARD SHAW

TRADITIONAL ORGANISATIONS

FORWARD-THINKING ORGANISATIONS

Use mass ads and recruitment agencies to call in potential recruits. Conduct pen/paper or online assessments (technical and psychometric), followed by traditional interviews (one-one or panel). Respond to people after a long process via letters or emails or not respond at all.

RECRUITMENT

Use innovative methods that take advantage of social-media, virtual techniques, referral software and job posting boards. Application tracking systems used so applicants get instant messages and responses, plus video and digital interviewing, blind auditions, skill challenges, etc.

Spend a couple of hours, a day, or even up to a week of presentations provided to group of recruits accompanied by a tour of the departments. May be given a pack that instructs them on certain guidelines and offer information about general administrative matters and the "who is who" of the organisation.

INDUCTION AND ONBOARDING

Carefully design engaging programmes using software that manages paperwork and creates individualized checklists, use HR solutions that offer get-to-know-you emails, coaching and sharing information in longer term onboarding programmes. Not a one-day or one-week event— a process. Pre-joining virtual tours, gamification, competitions and team exercises used.

Offer periodic feedback in quarterly, semi-annually or annual sessions. Use paper-based or online forms scored by managers. May include self-assessments. One interview to formalize the process, get signatures and approvals of scores attained and given. Discussion of developmental needs and reflections on KPIs achieved.

APPRAISAL

Evaluations through assessment centers, 360 and 720 degree methods, utilising continuous activity. Provide constant feedback and have replaced appraisals with career charting and growth.

Determine training needs based on HR plans and budgets approved with input from department heads. Outsource all training delivery and send employees to offsite programmes. Quota of minimal hours of formal learning. Training does not align with corporate needs and priorities.

PROMOTIONS, REWARDS, CAREER GROWTH

Opportunity to exercise influence, recognize individual achievements, provide personalized training. Give cross functional valuable experiences which add to personal growth and align with purpose at all times. Provide bite-size micro-learning. Use a combination of training delivery platforms—onsite and offsite. Use VR and AR in training. Provide strong coaching and mentoring engagement.

Recognise need for acknowledging employees on a consistent basis, thus retaining talent through alignment of personal and corporate purpose. Exiting employees interviewed for lessons learnt, analysis of company performance and other metrics related to good HR attraction/retention KPIs. Maintain relationships for ongoing loyalty and talent pool if needed for ad-hoc purpose. Value maintaining. Core value of turning exiting employees into potential ambassadors and loyal customers.

Don't anticipate the exit nor understand difference between healthy and unhealthy turnover due to lack of data gathering. Offer routine procedures in exit interviews, regular checklist being ticked and signed in interview format. No contact maintained or desired with leaving staff.

DECISIONS/MAKING CHOICES/CONFLICT

REFERENCES

1. Next Generation Study 2017, Price Water House Coopers International, 2017

2. Next Generation Study 2013, Price Water House Coopers International, 2013

3. Millennials at work Reshaping the workplace, PWC Survey, 2013

4. Workforce of the future - The Competing Forces Shaping 2030, PWC Global

5. The Deloitte Millennial Survey 2018, Deloitte, 2018.

6. Qudurat Wave II Study, AON Hewitt, 2013.

7. Net Impact Survey, Talent Report - What Worker Want, 2012.

8. Future Workplaces' Multiple Generations @ Work Survey, 2013.

9. 2018 Deloitte Millennial Survey - Millennials Disappointed in Business, Unprepared for Industry 4.0, Deloitte, 2018.

10. Millennial Behaviors & Demographics, Richard Sweeney, New Jersey Institute of Technology University Heights, Newark, December 22, 2006.

11. We are More Different than You Think, Insead, Emerging Markets Institute, The Head Foundation and Universum, 2018.

12. Entrepreneurial Creatives, Skeptical - The Truth about MENA Millennials, Chayme Samir, World Economic Forum, 2017

13. Characteristics of Millennials in the Workplace, Terri Klass and Judy Lindenberger, January 9, 2017

14. Who are the Millennials, Douglas Main, LiveScience Staff Writer, September 8, 2017

15. 8 Millennials' Traits you Should Know Before Hiring Them, Blogger Lydia Abbot

16. Stereotypes on Millennials and Why They are Wrong, Aisha Gani, The Guardian International, March 2016.

17. HR Re-Skilling: Top 3 Areas HR Pros Should Master Now, Dawn Burke, Industry Buzz, The Saba Blog, May 14, 2018

18. Millennials Think your Performance Review Sucks, Here is Why, by Kim Runyen based on TriNet Perform Survey, October 2015

19. Performance Reviews Drive One in Four Millennials to Search for a New Job or Call in Sick, TriNet Perform Study, October 2015.

20. 4 Companies that are Shaking up their Performance Review Process, Chris Rhatigan, Tiny Pulse, May 3, 2016

21. The 5 ways your Performance Review is Failing Millennials, Talent Guard.

22. 6 ways to Keep Millennials Engaged, Errand Solutions , January 2018.

23. From Millennials with Love: Young Professionals' Stories on Their Experience of Work, Ann-Victoire Pince, Upfront Publishing, October 2015

24. Millennials are Taking over the Workforce, Jeanette Settembre, Moneyish, April 2018

25. How To Harness The Power Of A Millennial Workforce, Kevin Kruse, Forbes, May 2017.

26. Millennials And Entitlement In The Workplace: The Good, The Bad, and the Ugly, Larry Alton, Forbes, November 2017.

27. Forget the Career Ladder, Millennials Are Taking the Elevator, Gabrielle Jackson, The Blog, May 2016

28. PeW Research - Millennials are the largest generation in the U.S. Labor force, Richard Fry, Pew Research Centre, April 2018

ABOUT THE AUTHORS

AMAL KOOHEJI

Amal has been on a journey of human capital and enterprise development for the past 25 years. She is the founder of Human Capital Advisory, a Bahrain-based firm specializing in designing schemes that aim to improve the productivity of individuals, organizations and nations. She enjoys passionate discussions, problem-solving and believes that change is the only path to growth. She thrives on controversy, and aims to instil passion and purpose in the fragment of organizations, their people, and the world at large. She is blessed with the support of a wonderful family, a network of dear friends from all age groups, and a wonderful social sphere on the beautiful and tiny island of Bahrain.

SAJEDA AL ASFOOR

Sajeda works in her passion domain in one of the leading public sector organisations in Bahrain. Her role revolves around running Human Capital development projects that strive to empower youth and prepare them for the labour market. She has led women empowerment projects locally and internationally followed by a fellowship in the UK, having spent most of her teenage years in youth societies and civic engagement programs. She is married to a supportive husband and is a loving mom to two beautiful children. Juggling a job and motherhood at the young age of 23 did not, however, stop her from binge watching all her favourite shows on Netflix.

www.ingramcontent.com/pod-product-compliance
Lightning Source LLC
Chambersburg PA
CBHW070425240526
45472CB00020B/1244